FAITH
It's God Given

by

Michael S B Reid

Alive UK

49 Coxtie Green Road
Pilgrims Hatch Brentwood
Essex CM14 5PS

Portions of this book are adapted from
Whose Faith Is It Anyway?
© 1990 Sharon Publications, England.

Copyright 2000, by Alive UK
Printed in England

ISBN 1 871367 30 1

DEDICATION

To Demos Shakarian, a true and faithful minister,
who introduced me to the wonderful things of God,

and

To Peter, Carolyn and friends, who helped so much
in compiling this book.

Contents

ORAL ROBERTS UNIVERSITY
With Dr Jerry Horner, then Dean of Theology, receiving a
Masters Degree in Practical Theology

Foreword

In this volume Bishop Michael Reid deals with a subject that lies at the very heart of the Christian's daily life. In this scriptural, balanced, and practical presentation, he shows that we are not only saved by faith, but we are to live and walk by faith, and we are to serve by faith. Those who master the art of living by true Biblical faith will witness miracles as a common experience. Some will find Bishop Reid's conclusions difficult to understand and apply, but they will receive a serious challenge to examine anew the Biblical evidence.

Dr Jerry Horner

Dr Horner has been a University professor for 36 years. He was the Dean of the School of Theology and Missions at Oral Roberts University for four years and is currently Dean of Theology at Peniel College of Higher Education. He was the founding Dean of the School of Divinity at Regent University and served as the Chairman of the Theology Departments at ORU and Southwest Baptist University. He is the author of many books, and is New Testament editor of THE SPIRIT-FILLED LIFE BIBLE.

*The late Archbishop Benson Idahosa,
Archbishop Earl Paulk and Bishop Reid at the
International Communion of Charismatic Churches
Convention held at Peniel Church, Brentwood, England.*

*With Richard Roberts, President of Oral Roberts
University, during a broadcast of his nightly TV show,
"The Healing Hour."*

Preface

I believe in miracles. To me they are as natural as breathing. When Jesus was on this earth He went about doing miracles - the cripples walked, deaf ears were opened, the blind received their sight, lives were transformed. He hasn't changed - He is eternally the same. I have a saying - *No miracles, no Jesus* - because the miracles which were the hallmark of His earthly ministry from the beginning, still operate today. I know, for with my own eyes I've witnessed what only God can do. I've seen Him reach out to those in hopeless situations and bring life and healing in the place of death and despair. If you need a miracle, you need Him - because where He is that supernatural power will always flow.

This book is written for those who are tired of struggling to believe, tired of the false faith emphasis which condemns and discourages. It is written for those who are prepared to realign their thinking on the Biblical basis for faith, which is *Christ in you, the hope of glory* (Colossians 1:27). When He comes in truth, all things are possible.

My theological background is very broad based. I was led to the Lord and received the baptism of the

Holy Spirit under the ministry of Demos and Rose Shakarian; greatly influenced by the first generation Quaker writings of George Fox, William Penn, James Naylor, Robert Barclay and Isaac Pennington; enriched by the Wesley brothers, George Whitfield and other Puritan writers; blessed by the books of Finney, Spurgeon, Count Zinzendorf and the Moravians; and inspired by the works of the Marechale, Smith Wigglesworth, Maria Woodworth-Etter, Aimee Semple Macpherson and Kathryn Kuhlman.

I enjoyed many years of rich fellowship and ministry with the late Archbishop Benson Idahosa, who was truly an outstanding apostle of faith of the twentieth century, a man who believed God and did exploits.

My life has been challenged by the work and writings of both Oral and Richard Roberts and I am honoured to count Dr T L Osborn as a friend and father in the faith.

I am grateful to Dr Judson Cornwall, for his wisdom, encouragement and friendship over many years. He also has been part of my shaping in God.

Now, from such a varied spiritual background, I want to offer you, my readers, a new insight into the life of faith. Perhaps you will find the message of this book a little controversial. I make no apology - it is my intention to shake your preconceived ideas and cherished idols so that *those things which cannot be shaken may remain* (Hebrews 12:27). However, my purpose is always and only to lift up Jesus, the *author and finisher of our faith* (Hebrews 12:2), and to magnify His name.

The only true basis of ministry is to do His will. We need to stop trying to coerce God into doing what we want and re-establish the heart cry, *Thy will be done on earth as it is in heaven* (Matthew 6:10). When we align ourselves with what God is doing, miracles happen; when He is the source, it's so, so easy!

It is my prayer that you will read with an open heart and that in reading you will find the richness and glory of grace in the face of Jesus Christ. Our God is a good God, who longs to bless and lift us up because He loves us.

*For God **so loved** the world, **that he gave** his only begotten Son, that whosoever believeth in him should not perish, but have everlasting life.* (John 3:16)

*For by grace are ye saved through faith; and that **not of yourselves: it is the gift of God.*** (Ephesians 2:8)

Everything begins and ends in Him.

Michael S B Reid
February 2000

Praying for the sick

1

A Miraculous Escape

With men this is impossible; but with God all things are possible.
(Matthew 19:26)

Several years ago, I met a woman at a conference in one of the largest cities of the USA. She had quite a story to tell!

The nightmare had begun about five years prior to this. Working as a cashier in a local supermarket, she and two male colleagues were suddenly held up at gunpoint by a desperate man just after they had closed for the night.

He failed to get any money so he forced the three into his car and drove off. Then,

Two men shot dead in front of her

to Julie's horror, he stopped in a lonely spot, made the men get out, and shot them dead in front of her.

Before she could fully take in what she had witnessed, the murderer pushed her back into the car, behind the driving wheel, and ordered her to drive off into the night.

It's not difficult to imagine the thoughts that would tumble through the mind in such a situation! Julie had the awful realisation that her own life hung in the balance. Then something rather strange happened.

Julie said that she prayed and felt the peace of God come over her. All the

She prayed and felt the peace of God

terror seemed to leave her; she stopped shaking and began to think rationally again.

Even stranger things were to happen to Julie that night as the car sped on through the countryside. As she gripped the wheel, she suddenly began to have visions of escaping by jumping out of the car. "I just kept seeing myself bailing out and I knew God was talking to me," she stated.

Suddenly she made up her mind, swerved the car to the right and threw herself out of the door before the killer could stop her. She hit the roadway and rolled behind the vehicle as it flashed past with its occupant struggling to regain control. As Julie continued to roll over and over she watched the lights of the car receding into the distance. Then to her horror, the car stopped and then began to reverse up the road in her direction.

Desperately, she struggled to her feet in an attempt to run, but her left ankle was broken and her foot dangled uselessly. She had no option but to crawl!

There she was, badly injured, in the middle of nowhere, trying to escape from a man who had already murdered two people and who had everything to gain by getting rid of the only material witness.

Fortunately, the orchard in which she found herself had been newly ploughed and furrowed that very day. The earth was soft, so scraping and digging with her hands, she buried herself in the soil, thankful for the covering darkness.

The assailant was not going to give up easily. He drove back and forth several times vainly searching for some sign of Julie. Then, to her relief, all was quiet, and she began to hope that he had finally gone. She decided to crawl back to the roadside and try to find help. But, to her astonishment, God spoke again, warning her that the killer was still around and that anyone she might turn to for help would face certain death as well.

Unable to rest, however, she thought of dragging herself across the orchard to some distant houses she had previously seen. Again, that insistent voice spoke:

"Listen to the dogs barking! He's there waiting for you! Don't go!" It seemed Julie had no choice but to lie quietly and wait for dawn.

She cowered in the earth trying to bury herself deeper but sure enough her tormentor returned. This time he was on a bicycle, systematically searching through the fields and the orchard. Would he never go?

It was a long night and all she could do was wait. But God had hidden her and as the sun rose the next morning she was safe and finally alone!

God had hidden her

Shortly after day-break, a man on a tractor started to plough the far end of the orchard. Julie was, by now, in a terrible physical condition - her shoulder was broken, her hand badly damaged, her ankle shattered, and in addition large areas of flesh were torn and lacerated after her crawl through the orchard.

Although it seemed that the killer had gone she was frightened of making too much noise in case he was still lurking around somewhere. So she waited in agony until the plough, which was making great loops of the field, came within reasonable distance, and then she waved to the driver. At first he thought it was merely a friendly greeting and he paid no attention. It was not until she tied her jersey to a stick and waved it frantically that he realised something was really wrong and came to her aid. "It was a wonderful moment," said Julie, "all the birds began to sing."

Julie had been rescued from her immediate nightmare but another test of courage still lay ahead. Her injuries, already severe after her jump from the car, had been aggravated by the events of the night. Rushed to hospital, surgeons at first doubted if they could save parts of her tortured body and gangrene was an immediate threat. She was on an intensive care programme for a month as the doctors fought to repair some of the damage.

Julie was confined to a wheelchair for six months and was to suffer years of bone and skin grafts. She had twelve operations in three years and became convinced that she had nothing to look forward to but a life of pain and physical handicap.

Then her family moved their home, under the police witness protection scheme, to another part of the country and started to attend the church where I was invited to minister one summer at a large convention.

Everyone was singing and I remember looking down and noticing Julie. She was sitting in a chair on the front row and was obviously in some discomfort and pain. I had no idea who she was or what had happened to her, but God spoke and told me He would heal her.

I left the platform and went and pulled her to her feet saying, "God's going to heal you right now."

She said, "What of?"

I said, "Everything!"

Then she just fell back to the floor under the power of God. A little later I saw her stir so I returned to help her up. It was useless! She fell back again, laughing and laughing.

After a further five or six minutes she calmed down. I left the platform again, put out my right hand and pulled her up. She leapt to her feet and began to run across the front of the meeting hall, leaping and jumping and waving both arms above her head, as she shouted, "I'm healed, I'm healed, I'm healed!" God had come! In His marvellous sovereign way, He had chosen Julie out of the congregation to demonstrate His wonderful love and power. She did not even have the faith to ask. But His faith performed the impossible. All Julie

His faith performed the impossible

had to do was to receive her healing and a lovely touch from the living God. Her foot, hand and shoulder had been miraculously and instantly healed! Later, doctors could not fathom out how fused bones could function freely. Today, fourteen years later, she is still healed and well.

When it's God's, faith it works!

Do you remember the man Jesus came to at the pool of Bethesda? As with Julie, Jesus came to him sovereignly. The Master's question was straight and to the point -

Wilt thou be made whole?

(John 5:6)

The man had been crippled for thirty-eight years, but in answer to Christ's question, he immediately gave excuses for remaining in his condition -

Sir, I have no man, when the water is troubled, to put me into the pool: but while I am coming, another steppeth down before me.

(John 5:7)

How often we give Jesus all the reasons why we can't have what He offers us. We make excuses instead of laying hold of Him. We might not speak them out but we certainly think them inside, don't we?

"Look, Lord, you don't understand, you haven't seen me over these years. You have no idea what I've been through. You don't know how I ended up in this state. No one understands me! I want to give You a good explanation of how I got here."

We go through all our yesterdays. We begin to tell how it was. This happened, that happened. We give all our reasons and we ignore

Do you want to be free?

the one and only question that Christ is concerned with. He doesn't care how we got there! He's concerned with only one thing. Do we want to remain in bondage or be free? His words to us are the same as He spoke to the man at the pool -

Wilt thou be made whole?

(John 5:6)

Have you noticed how Jesus ignored the man's answer and healed him anyway? He just told him to take up his bed and walk. That was the end of that! He paid no attention to anyone else. He came to do one miracle for one man who was in the middle of a crowd.

When Jesus came to Julie, He came to change her life! He already knew her yesterdays. He knew the man at the pool of Bethesda. He knows you!

You don't have to make any excuses, He doesn't need your explanations. He doesn't want to know your

Jesus knows *you!*

life history or what your mother and father did. It doesn't matter. You don't have to fight to believe. Our God of love has come in sovereign power - He'll believe for you! He will do it by His Power.

> *With men this is impossible; but with God all things are possible.*
>
> *(Matthew 19:26)*

It's so, so easy!!!

Praying for a sick infant in Lagos, Nigeria

Dr TL Osborn, Bishop LaDonna Osborn, Bishop Michael &
Rev Ruth Reid, Bishop Margaret Idahosa at a Ministers'
Convention in Benin City, Nigeria.

2

Miracles Belong To Him

And a great multitude followed him,
because they saw his miracles which he did
on them that were diseased.
(John 6:2)

Every miracle of Jesus belongs to Him alone, and the reasons He performs them are His to know.

Most of us spend our lives needlessly struggling. We try to find the key that will unlock the door to that faith we're convinced we should have, but which so often eludes us. People are told, "All you've got to do is this or that, then God has got to move." But the truth is, He hasn't! God never has to do anything because man demands it, nor because he has met certain criteria. There is no formula! God is God, and He'll do what He wills, how He wills, when He wills and through whom He wills.

Man wants an explanation for everything: with his finite mind he concocts great theories about the infinite God and His ways. But the simple truth is that our God is a God of mysteries, and that defies all human logic and understanding.

> *For my thoughts are not your thoughts, neither are your ways my ways, saith the LORD.*
>
> *For as the heavens are higher than the earth, so are my ways higher than your ways, and my thoughts than your thoughts.*
>
> *(Isaiah 55:8-9)*

> *Canst thou by searching find out God? canst thou find out the Almighty unto perfection?*
>
> *It is high as heaven; what canst thou do? deeper than hell; what canst thou know? The measure thereof is longer than the earth, and broader than the sea.*
>
> *(Job 11:7-9)*

Amy Carmichael once wrote these words:-

> A centipede was happy till
> One day a toad, in fun, said
> "Pray which leg goes after which?"
> Which strained his mind to such a pitch
> He lay distracted in a ditch
> Considering how to run.

I think that's what some theories on faith did for me - they left me confused and totally immobilised!

Let's just accept the fact that God will move as He desires, and that His miracles and His power belong to Him alone.

> **His miracles and His power belong to Him alone**

In John 6 we have the familiar story of the feeding of the five thousand. We read that Jesus came to Philip and asked him,

> *Whence shall we buy bread, that these may eat?*
> *(John 6:5)*

Jesus already knew what He was going to do, but He asked the question to prove Philip. He was really saying - "Philip, I want to find out what is going on inside you. Where are we going to find food for all this multitude? How would you cope with the problem? What are you thinking, Philip?"

Philip's answer was natural enough -

> *Two hundred pennyworth of bread is not sufficient for them.*
>
> *(John 6:7)*

But notice that he replied to a question which Jesus had never even asked. The Master wanted to know where bread could be bought, not how much was needed. Philip didn't even consider the solution, because he was blinded by the immensity of the problem itself.

Very often when we come to the Lord, we don't consider the source of supply, the fount of all life. Our human logic takes over, and all we see is the magnitude of the need.

Have you ever sat down before God and tried to sort out your life? A preacher makes an appeal and you really want to get your heart right with God. You decide one day you'll make a list of all the things that need to be changed. After you've written 30 pages you think, "I'm quitting! Lord, there's just too much wrong with me!" Your heart is so overwhelmed with the enormity of the problems, that you lose sight of the source of supply.

God is the source of supply

Philip didn't respond to Jesus in faith and, usually, neither do we. God wants to feed our souls, but we come to Him with total unbelief and tell Him how impossible it is for Him to meet our needs.

So if Philip showed no faith, what of the others?

If anything Andrew was even worse! He was going to throw out the only little provision they had -

> *There is a lad here, which hath five barley loaves, and two small fishes: but what are they among so many?*
>
> *(John 6:9)*

Have you ever thought about that little lad?

The boy had perceived that in Jesus there was something beyond the natural, so he offered all he had, five loaves and two small fishes. Andrew would have given them back and sent him away. The boy had faith, but not Andrew.

There were thousands of people thronging that mountainside, so how did Andrew know just what the boy carried in his basket? There were other baskets there - later they were able to fill twelve with the fragments that were left over. But this one was special because it was offered.

Here was a lad who came to Jesus with the only thing he had. It wasn't much and he knew it. But he saw the great need and he said, "Lord, You know this is all I have. Please take it! It's Yours." Somehow he realised that if Jesus would only take his small gift and bless it, so much could happen. He came and gave all he possessed to the King of Kings. That was the heart of the lad.

Jesus took the loaves and fishes and commanded the men to sit down. Then He looked up to Heaven ... and everything changed.

"Philip, this is where it all comes from - it comes from heaven."

He blessed the bread, broke it, and as the disciples gave it out, there was more than enough for everyone. And sitting watching the miracle was one little boy who could never be the same again. He understood that his insignificant little gift was the very thing that had caused all the glory to be revealed. Five thousand men, besides women and children, ate and were filled that day, and they all acknowledged the King of Glory.

The trouble with most people is that what they have they won't give. This boy gave all he had to be multiplied by the source of life. His eyes were on Jesus, not on the size of the problem. He understood a secret that very few are able to see - God takes the things that are not, the insignificant things, the things that are given from the heart, and He blesses those offerings abundantly.

> **God takes the things that are not and blesses abundantly**

Andrew scoffed at the gift, considering it too small to be of any use and when the child heard Andrew speak his heart fell. Then suddenly Jesus was telling everyone to sit down and the boy fixed his eyes again on the face of the One he loved. He had followed Him to the mountainside, now he waited to see what the Lord would do.

Afterwards what a story he had to tell! I am sure Andrew gave him one of the baskets full of fragments to take home to his mother. But the real gift he received that day was the gift of faith in Christ from the fount of life Himself!

That lad was willing to give.

Could you believe the Master, that He could take what you have into His own hands, bless it, break it, and use it to feed multitudes? No, you won't feed them. No, you won't even be noticed. We're never told that the little boy was even thanked. He didn't get the glory, because that belongs to God alone. But he went home a different person because he had met with Jehovah Jireh, the source of all supply.

I've often thought about this miracle. If I had been in the multitude, I would have wanted some of the newly created bread! I wonder how it actually multiplied. I'm sure the disciples walked around with proud looks on their faces - "Of course, we knew He could do it all along!"

But, if we're honest, it's only afterwards that we find it easy to believe. Until then we know that He's able but we can't help wondering if He will!

I've learned a secret - it's better not to ask questions, but to wait for Him. Pray, yes, and wait until He comes. The miracle of Life happens at the point when the living reality of His presence is there. Then we can drink of that Source - that heavenly Source - and that which seems impossible is done in a moment.

I don't come to God with demands, I don't come saying, "Lord, You've got to." I come with a heart of trust which declares, "Lord, I know You're able, and I just bring myself to You and put myself in Your hands."

> **It's not my believing, it's His believing that creates life**

I don't look at the problem, I look at the wonderful source of all life - Jesus my Lord! In simplicity I lay myself at His feet and say, "Lord, You are the source who never fails!"

It's not my believing, it's His believing that creates life.

When He died on Calvary's tree and took my sin into his own body, I had nothing to do with it. I wasn't there, I hadn't even been born. But His faith and love took my sin into Himself and He paid the penalty for it two thousand years ago. I did nothing. He did it all.

God is coming to draw out a people for Himself who are going to be totally given over to living and dying for Him. Those who will put everything on the altar unreservedly and say, "Lord, I want You to be Lord in truth. I want You to so captivate my heart and soul that my only source is You - not my own knowledge, not my own strength, not my own ability, but You."

Part of the ministry of the church of which I am a pastor, is a school, widely recognised as one of the top private academic institutions in England. We were visited on one occasion by another minister who wanted to know how it all functioned. After looking around he bombarded me with questions - "Where does this come from? What do you do about that? How do you arrange that?"

I had no blueprint to offer him. So I simply said, "You can have all the right methods, all the best ways of doing things. You could copy that which God has shown us but it wouldn't necessarily work for you. For we have found that He was the one who brought it about and if He doesn't do it, it won't happen."

The truth is that Jesus is the Source of whatever He wants you to do. So you need to find Him and align yourself with His will. As He lived, so we should live. His only purpose and desire was to fulfil the will of His Father. His was a life of simple obedience.

Then answered Jesus and said unto them, Verily, verily, I say unto you, The Son can do nothing of himself, but what he seeth the Father do: for what things soever he doeth, these also doeth the Son likewise.
(John 5:19)

Then said I, Lo, I come (in the volume of the book it is written of me,) to do thy will, O God.
(Hebrews 10:7)

We find that way of living so difficult to accomplish. Our human hearts demand reasons, explanations; we want to know how it all works.

Jesus wants to be the source of all for you. He wants you to learn how to feed on Him and draw from Him all that you need. He wants you to give up trust in yourself and

> **The only reality is what He does, the way He does it**

see the only reality is what He does, the way He does it. Remember, miracles belong to Him. In your heart, it will be His miracle, if you make room for Him.

With men this is impossible; but with God all things are possible.

(Matthew 19:26)

With Archbishop Benson Idahosa at Peniel Church

Deep in discussion with Dr TL Osborn during a Miracle Conference held at Peniel Church.

3

All Things Are Possible

... all things are possible to him that believeth.
(Mark 9:23)

The ninth chapter of Mark records an intriguing episode in the ministry of Jesus.

Master, I have brought unto thee my son, which hath a dumb spirit;

And wheresoever he taketh him, he teareth him: and he foameth, and gnasheth with his teeth, and pineth away: and I spake to thy disciples that they should cast him out; and they could not.

(Mark 9:17-18)

What a desperate cry there was in that father's heart! He had come seeking help and the disciples had failed him. Jesus had not been there. He had gone away with Peter, James and John into a high mountain. While the glory of His transfiguration was revealed before their eyes, the nine remaining disciples had had to face this poor man with his tormented child.

I wonder how they felt! I am sure they prayed and shouted, begged and demanded, wept and rebuked ... but nothing had happened.

In the early years of my Christian life, I moved in power ministry. People in need would come and I prayed with them. Sometimes nothing I did worked. I tried in every possible way. I prayed, I struggled and I prayed again. I knew that God could do it, but I also knew that He wasn't doing it!

There were other times when the miracles happened straightaway - because Jesus was there. But on this occasion the disciples had been on their own. To make matters worse, a great multitude gathered around them and the Scribes and Pharisees were not slow to take advantage of their embarrassment.

> **Miracles happened because Jesus was there**

I can imagine how they taunted them - "So you think you're smart do you? See, it doesn't work! You can't even meet the needs of a little boy. Your leader isn't as wonderful as you thought, is He? We warned you that He was a heretic. Perhaps now you'll listen."

The Pharisees were jubilant! This was the opportunity they had been waiting for. Up until this time Jesus had proved more than a match for them. Somehow he had always managed to return their carefully aimed questions with an authority and wisdom which left them speechless. But now they reckoned that they had finally outwitted Him. At last, all the people would see that the common carpenter from Nazareth was nothing better than an impostor! His claims were false and so was His power!

It's strange how the enemy always overstretches the mark. The mockery of the critics was short-lived, for Jesus returned, silenced them, and took command of the situation.

By this time the poor father's faith was at a very low ebb. Yet a little spark of hope rekindled as he saw Jesus. He spoke out from the crowd to explain what had been happening - the problem, the suffering, the coming, and the crushing disappointment of the disciples' failure. He could no longer believe that his son would be made whole but perhaps Jesus could do something, anything, to alleviate their terrible situation. If He could stop the lad from being thrown into the fire, that would be tremendous. If he could prevent him from being totally destroyed, that would be wonderful.

Jesus said:-

> *If thou canst believe, all things are*
> *possible to him that believeth.*
> *(Mark 9:23)*

I was looking at this scripture and God said to me, "Have you read it?" I replied, "Yes, Lord, I've read it." He spoke once more, "No, have you really read it?" I looked again and then the truth dawned on me.

He was saying, "Can you believe that all things are possible to Him who believes." He didn't ask the man to believe that his son would be delivered. He asked him to have faith in the One who was able to deliver. The scales dropped from my eyes! I thought "Lord, I've always struggled to believe for the thing I need, and I've never seen this before."

Have faith in the One who was able to deliver

So often we fight to muster up faith, and like the disciples we fail miserably. People are told, "If you really believe for your healing, you'll be healed." But I say, "Not so. Believe Him who is able. Believe Him who believes. He never doubts. He never fears. He never loses faith. All things are possible to Him. All we have to do is believe in Him who can do everything. He is the Answer."

> *And straightway the father of the child cried out, and said with tears, Lord, I believe;*
>
> *(Mark 9:24)*

But he didn't stop there. He prayed a prayer - one which I believe we all, if we're honest, would have prayed - *"... help thou mine unbelief."*

Jesus didn't condemn him. He didn't require him to rise up in mighty faith and claim deliverance for his son. He knew what was going to happen. He knew His Heavenly Father's will. He rebuked the foul spirit, commanding it to leave the boy for ever.

> *And the spirit cried, and rent him sore, and came out of him: and he was as one dead; ...*
>
> *But Jesus took him by the hand, and lifted him up; and he arose.*
>
> *(Mark 9:26-27)*

Why couldn't the disciples perform that miracle? Why was everything so different when Jesus came? They had just lost sight of their need of the Master. He alone had both the faith and the power to set the boy free.

> **He alone had both the faith and the power to set the boy free**

The gifts of the Spirit belong to the Spirit of God. They're His and they function in Him. God can flow through an individual as He desires, but He will never impart to us the power to do anything of ourselves. He wants us to be ever conscious of our total dependence upon Him. A man who claims the precious gifts of God as his own possession is a man who has dethroned Christ.

Shortly after our second daughter was born, it became apparent that she was very ill. She had a chromosome deficiency and the doctors told us that she would never develop normally. Their advice was to put her in a suitable institution.

I remember the agony of that time. I believed that God could heal her, I knew that He was able. But I needed help for my unbelief. I needed a word from Him.

One day the Lord came to me with a question,

"Do you love your daughter?"

I said, "Of course I do, Father."

He came the second time, "Do you love your daughter?"

Again, I replied, "Of course, Lord".

Then He spoke words which I can never forget, "How much more do I love her, as her Heavenly Father."

In that moment, I knew she was going to be healed. And twenty-four years later it's still a thrill to testify to how God was faithful to His word. From the instant He spoke she began to get well. He worked a miracle and today she's a normal happy adult, having gained a degree in historical studies and is librarian of Peniel College of Higher Education.

God wants to do things you never dreamed were possible. Your heart, your mind and your spirit tell you it can never be. But Jesus comes and declares, "If you can believe that all things are possible to the One who believes - it shall be."

When God intervenes in a life it's not because we've earned it, or because we deserve it, or because we've found a special formula. He intervenes because He's the Lord of Glory, and He's chosen to do so. He's chosen to reveal His love and grace. He's chosen to deliver us and meet our deepest needs.

The father's unbelief was ended when he took his son home. He went to every neighbour, "See, my son - he's back. He's well. Jesus did it all."

Jesus has absolute faith in the complete and perfect atonement He made on Calvary's tree. He has faith in the fact that when His back was scourged by those terrible cords, your healing was purchased. The right for Him to heal you was bought that day.

Jesus has faith that when He poured out His blood He was purchasing your life, your pardon and your cleansing. He knew you were going to be delivered and made whole.

Jesus believed two thousand years ago and He's never doubted. His faith is the faith we need - not our faith, but the faith of God.

> **When His faith comes, all the struggles end**

When His faith comes, all the struggles end. We simply trust in Him, that He is able to do it.

You don't have to live for years under bondage. God says there is a Deliverer. He delivers you so that the light of God's countenance can flood your heart and your soul, so that the love of God can quicken you, make you alive and set you free.

> *Shall the prey be taken from the mighty, or the lawful captive delivered?*
>
> *But thus saith the LORD, Even the captives of the mighty shall be taken away, and the prey of the terrible shall be delivered ...*
> *(Isaiah 49:24,25)*

Lord, how can it be? All things are possible to Him that believes! God can do anything ... anything but fail!

*A meeting at Peniel Church packed
with people praising God.*

*With Oral Roberts, Chancellor of Oral Roberts
University, at a Regents meeting in Tulsa, Oklahoma.*

4

The Lion Of The Tribe Of Judah Has Prevailed

... the lion of the tribe of Judah..
hath prevailed..
(Rev 5:5)

I remember a very special night, some years ago. As I slept, all hell seemed to break loose upon me. I began to fight and to struggle. I fought all night long. When I awoke next morning, I had the terrible feeling that hell had invaded me. For the whole day, it stirred within me.

The next night as I went to sleep, hell seemed to envelop me again - and again I fought and fought. It was as though the darkness was going to overwhelm me and take me down. I began to cry, "Lord, save me."

All of a sudden, I heard a mighty shout, and heaven opened. Jesus came, and I began to stamp and trample on those forces of evil. I heard the angels break forth into a triumphant song, it resounded through the heavenlies, "The Lion of the Tribe of Judah has prevailed over all His enemies." Oh, my heart got so full of life! In that moment I knew He'd done it! I knew He'd conquered! His power and glory flooded my soul! His is the glory and the victory!

> **The Lion of the Tribe of Judah has prevailed over all His enemies**

I woke up with the song of the angels in my heart. There was the certainty that my Jesus, the glorious Man of Calvary, had triumphed. I knew it. In the depths of my spirit something that changed me had been brought to birth. "The Lion of the tribe of Judah has prevailed over all His enemies" - every single one of them! Glory to His wonderful name!

That experience energised my soul. It quickened my being and thrilled my heart, vitalising my spirit with His faith. I remember going into our first church service after this happened. I felt as though I wanted to burst with joy. I knew that heaven was still rejoicing in that glorious victory. Jesus came. He began to sweep over the congregation and everywhere people fell under the power of God. It was like a sickle going through a field of ripe grain.

I began to have new insights into Biblical truths. My eyes had seen dimly, but suddenly they were opened, and the wonder of this divine revelation filled my heart. Jesus had come to do a marvellous work, to build His church, to set His people free.

> *Behold, my servant, whom I uphold;*
> *mine elect, in whom my soul delighteth;*
> *I have put my spirit upon him: he shall*
> *bring forth judgment to the Gentiles.*
>
> *He shall not fail nor be discouraged,*
> *till he have set judgment in the earth:*
> *and the isles shall wait for his law.*
> *(Isaiah 42:1,4)*

I was always taught, in my early Christian life, that judgment begins at the house of God, and that therefore we should fear and quake. It was really such a negative understanding. But then I started to comprehend what the judgment really is. It's wonderful. It's a judgment on our enemies, on the sins which pull us down and bring death within.

We fight and struggle against the wrong motives and desires which threaten to destroy our souls. Yet somehow we can't do anything effective about them until He comes. We find ourselves totally overwhelmed and ensnared by the inner forces of our carnal minds.

For to be carnally minded is death; but
to be spiritually minded is life and peace.

Because the carnal mind is enmity
against God: for it is not subject to the
law of God, neither indeed can be.
(Romans 8:6-7)

Well, here's the good news!

Well, here's the good news! Judgment is coming! Our God has come to deal with all that opposes His life in us, because He loves us. He comes to set us free because He is God, and He has come to save us.

I the Lord have called thee in
righteousness, and will hold thine hand,
and will keep thee, and give thee for
a covenant of the people, for a light of
the Gentiles;

To open the blind eyes, to bring out
the prisoners from the prison, and them
that sit in darkness out of the prison house.
(Isaiah 42:6-7)

Jesus was ordained to bring those that sit in darkness out of the prison house - the prison house of fears, of doubts and of all bondages. Jesus has come to bring you right out! Not just out of your little cell, but right out of your prison house. He's come to bring you forth to life in Him.

As I dreamed, I saw in my own spirit all the prisoners just walking out after Him. Can you imagine following Him right out into the light, dancing in your new-found freedom, and knowing that you need never go back? That's our Jesus - that's what He's come to do for you.

What deliverance is it if you have light, but you remain in your cell? Or if you escape your cell, but stay in the prison house? He says, "No! It doesn't have to be that way - I've come to bring you right out of the house of your fathers, out of the house of Adam, and into the house of Christ."

Now that is victory!

You might be thinking that all I'm doing is giving you just another

> ## He comes to lead the prisoners forth

doctrine, and that if you believe it enough, it'll work. No! No! No! If He doesn't bring you out, you're not going to get out. But you have to be prepared to abandon your prison cell. You can't demand His blessing whilst you cling to your chains. He comes to lead the prisoners forth.

> *Long my imprisoned spirit lay,*
> *Fast bound in sin and nature's night,*
> *Thine eye diffused a quickening ray,*
> *I woke, the dungeon flamed with light.*
> *My chains fell off, my heart was free,*
> *I rose, went forth, and followed Thee.*

The freedom God gives is real. I can identify with those wonderful words of Wesley. If you have chains, you're in the dungeon. Jesus came to set the prisoner free, to bring you out of your bondage, and to give you liberty. He'll do it. The mountains of sin in your life will be brought low. The mountains that you can't conquer, the mountains that seem to rise up ever higher - God says He will deal with them. Those lusts, those evil desires, those fears that plague you, He says that He'll bring them down.

I love a God like that! You can't do it, but He will! He says He will.

That's why He bore your sin on Calvary's tree - to cleanse you and make you free. He didn't give you a revelation of Himself so that you could say for the rest of your life, "Lord, I believe that one day you'll deliver me."

I don't believe that God desires you to live in sin or bondage any longer. I don't believe it brings glory to God for His people to be downtrodden, tormented and trapped. It's a reproach, and the Mighty Lion of Judah has declared:-

> *... I will no more make you a reproach among the heathen:*
>
> *(Joel 2:19)*

Years ago I explained the gospel to two college students and they just laughed at me. They said it couldn't be that easy. The world thinks it's too simple, to them it's foolishness. Christians say it's tough to leave your sin. Preachers claim it's tough to abandon those drives within; and most of all it's tough to give up the self-life. How ridiculous they are!

Jesus, that great Christ of God, has come. He's come to be your salvation, to live His life within you. There is deliverance in Zion and when He finds you, you

> **He's come to be to live His life within you - Your life for His**

will have new life in Him. He'll transform every part of your being into the glorious image of Himself. It's a glorious process which will continue for the rest of your life.

> *But we all, with open face beholding*
> *as in a glass the glory of the Lord, are*
> *changed into the same image from*
> *glory to glory, even as by the Spirit*
> *of the Lord.*
>
> *(2 Corinthians 3:18)*

You have to leave everything for this. You have to give up your worthless ambitions, your pride, your self-esteem. Everything has to go. That is the price - total surrender. Your life for His. Self-denial is costly. It doesn't happen when we are first birthed into God but it becomes a way of life for those who will go on to full maturity in Him.

Few choose to walk this road; few desire the way of the Cross. Jesus Himself said:-

If any man will come after me, let him deny himself, and take up his cross, and follow me.

For whosoever will save his life shall lose it: and whosoever will lose his life for my sake shall find it.

(Matthew 16: 24-25)

For those who are prepared to pay that price, such a small price, what a glory awaits!

"The Lion of the Tribe of Judah has prevailed over all his enemies." I believed it when I first heard that song ringing through the portals of heaven. I still believe it! God has made it part of my being.

Fear not, O land; be glad and rejoice: for the Lord will do great things.

And it shall come to pass, that whosoever shall call on the name of the LORD shall be delivered: for in mount Zion and in Jerusalem shall be deliverance, as the LORD hath said, and in the remnant whom the LORD shall call.

(Joel 2:21,32)

All over the nations, all over the world, God is raising up a people. They are a different people, very different. A people with surrender in their hearts; a people who know the delivering power of a delivering God; a people willing in the day of His power. That day is now. Right now!

"The Lion of the Tribe of Judah has prevailed over all his enemies."

It is finished!

David Gregg, healed of chronic sciatica
(see page 131 for Miracle story)

5

He Will Do It

When he was come down from the
mountain, great multitudes followed him.
And, behold, there came a leper and
worshipped him, saying, Lord, if thou wilt,
thou canst make me clean.
(Matthew 8:1-2)

Everyone of us comes to a place at some point where we ask God, "Lord, we know you can, but will You? I know you have the power to meet every need, but will you let that power flow to me?" And when Jesus was on earth, there was a leper with the same cry.

> **Lord we know you can, but will you?**

Has it ever struck you in this account, how strange it was that the leper was in that great multitude? At that time, a leper was totally ostracised from society.

He was shut out. The Mosaic law made it quite clear:-

> *Command the children of Israel that*
> *they put out of the camp every leper ...*
> *(Numbers 5:2)*

> *All the days wherein the plague shall be*
> *in him he shall be defiled; he is unclean:*
> *he shall dwell alone; without the camp*
> *shall his habitation be.*
> *(Leviticus 13:46)*

But this man had found a way through to Jesus. He had come right to where Jesus was. He fell down and worshipped Him saying,

> *... Lord, if thou wilt, thou canst make me*
> *clean.*
> *(Matthew 8:2)*

It's the question that rises in many hearts, "I know You can, but will You? I know that You can deliver me from sin, I know that You can break the bondages in my life, I know you can heal me, I know that You can do wonderful things - but will You?"

Jesus answered the leper, but His answer was prophetically given for every generation that was to come. He revealed His heart so beautifully in two words - *"I will."*

He will. I believe it with all my heart and soul.

In Scripture, leprosy speaks of sin and bondage. It's a biblical picture. It speaks of being cast out and of having no rights; it speaks of having no entrance, no way of approaching. Yet somehow, this leper managed to come just near enough to fall down and worship at the feet of the Saviour. There he found the miracle he had so earnestly desired. As Jesus touched him and spoke the words of life to his heart, immediately the leprosy was cleansed.

One of the most difficult things for the human heart is to come to honesty - honesty with ourselves, honesty with our brethren,

> **One of the most difficult things for the human heart is to come to honesty**

but most of all honesty with God. This leper had to make an open confession. He had to admit that he was a leper in spite of the rejection which could accompany that knowledge! The disease carried such terrible consequences that I'm sure many times he had tried to convince himself that it was all a mistake. He had attempted to hide it from himself and when that was no longer possible, he had continued the pretence before other people.

He must have heard the stories of the Man of Galilee, of the miracles He was performing for so many, and somehow a little spark of faith kindled in his heart. He began to hope that grace might touch him too.

Slowly, he reached a place of definition. What a turmoil there must have been in his mind as he weighed the options. He could choose to maintain the charade for as long as possible or to cast himself on the mercy of the Saviour, revealing the horrible secret which was eating away at his flesh. He had hidden it for so long, and now he would have to let everyone know, whatever the consequences.

But his need was greater than that haunting fear of exposure. In the end, he didn't really care what anyone thought; he knew he had only one hope left. His name was Jesus, this miracle worker from Galilee.

We're just the same as that leper. It's easy to put on a show, to have an outward goodness, an outward conformity. We try to hide our sin with the robe of our religious forms and ideas. We want to appear spiritual and we're so fearful of losing face, so fearful of rejection. Endless excuses hurtle through our thoughts - What if it doesn't work? What if He refuses? What if it isn't His will?

But the glorious Lamb of God has made a way for us. No matter how deep the leprosy, no matter how great the disfigurement, there is an immediate cleansing available.

His answers to our questions are clear - "If you have chains, I'll break them; if you have bondages, I'll loose them. I'll do it. I will."

> **If you have chains, I'll break them; if you have bondages, I'll loose them. I'll do it. I will.**

Shall the prey be taken from the mighty, or the lawful captive delivered?

But thus saith the LORD, Even the captives of the mighty shall be taken away, and the prey of the terrible shall be delivered: for I will contend with him that contendeth with thee, and I will save thy children.

(Isaiah 49:24-25)

It's true. Jesus came to save us. He came with that purpose. By the pre-determination of God, He came to burst our bonds asunder.

We simply have to come to Him with truth in our hearts and cry, "Lord, I want to be clean, will You cleanse me?"

He'll say, "I will" - and He'll do it. He'll break those chains. He'll tear them off with a fury directed not against us, but against the bondages which bind us. He hates them.

Our God is a Man of War. Our God is one who rises up with vengeance against the enemies of our souls which seek to twist, torment, wound and hurt. He comes to break their power because His is a love which destroys anything that would destroy us.

> *The LORD is a man of war: the LORD is his name ...*
>
> *Thy right hand, O LORD, is become glorious in power: thy right hand, O LORD, hath dashed in pieces the enemy.*
>
> *And in the greatness of thine excellency thou hast overthrown them that rose up against thee: thou sentest forth thy wrath, which consumed them as stubble.*
>
> *(Exodus 15:3, 6-7)*
>
> *... for he that toucheth you toucheth the apple of his eye.*
>
> *(Zechariah 2:8)*

Jesus went into the temple. He took whipcords and He drove out the money changers, overturning their tables. He hated to see His Father's house defiled, the place which should have been His habitation used for the selfish purposes of evil men.

> *And His disciples remembered that it was written, The zeal of thine house hath eaten me up.*
>
> *(John 2:17)*

Our Jesus has never changed

Our Jesus has never changed. That same zeal can be directed against the enemies of our souls, the bondages in our lives, right now! He comes to deliver the captive and set the prisoner free. He comes with a shout and a declaration, **"I WILL."**

We know He can. We all know in our minds that the Lord can do anything. But for many of us that intellectual belief has not yet been translated into a practical reality. We won't step out and say, "Right, Lord, I know you can. I believe you can. Now, will You? **Right Now!!"**

It's then that we have to drop all our defenses and abandon our hiding places. What's really working inside is going to be revealed. It's a matter of coming to honesty.

The leper came with worship, and one of the main elements of worship is truth:-

... true worshippers shall worship the Father in spirit and in truth: for the Father seeketh such to worship him.

(John 4:23)

His worship was speaking the truth to the Master; he had to make known the need he had worked so hard to conceal.

Will we come out of the multitude?

The real question is - will we come out of the multitude? Will we deny every doubt and every fear, and come to meet with the King of Kings, casting ourselves before Him with that cry, "Lord, will You?"

He has already declared His answer for every generation, and it applies for all eternity. God says, **"I WILL."**

On that day when Jesus came down from the mountain great multitudes of people followed Him. One leper was healed. I'm sure that there were many people with many different needs, but the Bible records just one who was prepared to admit his problem and ask for healing. The rest left, untouched and unchanged.

There are many who come for salvation but they still love their sin. They don't want to give it up. They say, "Lord, take this bondage out of my life," but they don't really mean it. And while there's that reluctance within to let go, God says, "No." He will never violate the will. He will never compel us to come to Him.

I remember one girl's testimony at the end of a series of camp meetings when God had moved in a glorious way. She said that for years she had prayed for God to set her free, but deep down inside she never really wanted it. Suddenly the light broke forth in her soul, and for the first time she meant it with all her being.

Then, it happened. She said, "I'm free, it's gone!" Of course it had. Like the leper, she had come to that place of self exposure, and in doing so she found the Saviour.

The Scriptures make it quite clear that as a man

> *... thinketh in his heart, so is he*
> *(Proverbs 23:7)*

We sin in the imagination. In the innermost heart we think the sins that we would never do outwardly. But Jesus has come to clean up the inside as well as the outside. In His infinite love and mercy He will cleanse and release us.

> **He is no fool who gives up that which he cannot keep to gain that which he cannot lose**

William Penn, that great revivalist preacher of the early Quakers, once said, "He is no fool who gives up that which he cannot keep to gain that which he cannot lose."

These words carry an eternal truth and an eternal warning. Many Christians live as though they were going to remain on this earth forever. They live as though they have all the time in the world. The truth is that time is running out, the end is near.

You may be saying, "I gave my heart and life to Jesus years ago. What has this to do with me?" You know, the leper was in the multitude, and so often within the church there are those whose greatest needs remain unmet. There seems to be almost a conspiracy of silence with regard to need in the life of a believer, under the misapprehension that acknowledgement of need would destroy faith. Many ministers seem afraid to challenge church members with the necessity to repent and change their lives. They forget that God hates hypocrisy. His kingdom is of the heart, not of an outward conformity.

> *Your new moons and your appointed feasts*
> *my soul hateth: they are a trouble unto*
> *me; I am weary to bear them.*
>
> *And when ye spread forth your hands,*
> *I will hide mine eyes from you: yea,*
> *when ye make many prayers, I will not*
> *hear: your hands are full of blood.*
>
> *Wash you, make you clean; put away*
> *the evil of your doings from before*
> *mine eyes; cease to do evil.*
>
> *(Isaiah 1:14-16)*

Pretence locks us out from deliverance.

> *Thine habitation is in the midst of*
> *deceit; through deceit they refuse to*
> *know me, saith the LORD.*
>
> *(Jeremiah 9:6)*

Pretence locks us out from deliverance

Leper, are you prepared to identify yourself? Or are you going to slink back into the multitude and hide? Are you going to be one who just looks on and wonders? Or are you honest enough to admit the truth within?

In that great host of people, the leper was the only one who truly wanted to be clean, who was prepared to admit his condition.

If you will open up your heart, He'll do the same for you

There was a cry in his heart. Jesus heard that cry, reached out and touched him. And if you will open up your heart, He'll do the same for you.

Come now, and let us reason together, saith the LORD: though your sins be as scarlet, they shall be as white as snow; though they be red like crimson, they shall be as wool.

If ye be willing and obedient, ye shall eat the good of the land:

(Isaiah 1:18-19)

His answer hasn't changed; His promise is forever true. Jesus says "I will, be thou clean!"

Amanda Bucket, well on her way to recovery from ME which had left her bedridden for 10 years
(see page 137 for Miracle story)

6

From Death Into Life

The hand of the LORD was upon me, and carried me out in the spirit of the LORD, and set me down in the midst of the valley which was full of bones,

And caused me to pass by them round about: and, behold, there were very many in the open valley; and, lo, they were very dry.
(Ezekiel 37:1-2)

God took his servant, Ezekiel, to a strange place, a valley of dry bones, a valley of death. He asked him to look out into that scene of silent hopelessness - bones, sun bleached, dusty and dry. All vestige of life had disappeared, and death reigned.

Then He asked him an even stranger question:-

Son of man, can these bones live?
(Ezekiel 37:3)

As Ezekiel surveyed that valley seemingly without hope, as he gazed on the utter desolation, the only answer which he could give was:-

O Lord God, thou knowest.
(Ezekiel 37:3)

In my own life and ministry I have found that time and again those same words rise in my heart. I talk to people in desperate situations, people with mixed-up lives, mixed-up hearts, mixed-up souls. I see the death and dryness within, and all I can say is, "O Lord, you know. Unless you quicken and make alive, nothing can be done, it's hopeless!"

But God had brought his servant, Ezekiel, to this place of death, not just to present a challenge but to fulfil it.

He spoke these words through the mouth of the prophet:-

Thus saith the Lord GOD unto these
bones; Behold, I will cause breath to
enter into you, and ye shall live:

*And I will lay sinews upon you, and will
bring up flesh upon you, and cover you
with skin, and put breath in you, and ye
shall live; and ye shall know that I am
the LORD.*

(Ezekiel 37:5-6)

**His word is
life and power.
Nothing can stop it.**

It was the declaration of the Living God, the Creator of heaven and earth. His word is life and power. Nothing can stop it. At His command sicknesses flee; the devil's hold is broken; graves open; the chains of death snap.

Even as he spoke out the words in obedience, Ezekiel beheld the miracle:-

*... and the breath came into them, and
they lived, and stood up upon their
feet, an exceeding great army.*

(Ezekiel 37:10)

God recruits His army in the valley of dry bones. He comes to those who have plumbed the depths of hopelessness and self-despair; those who will acknowledge in truth the dryness and barrenness within; those who will declare:-

*Our bones are dried, and our hope is
lost: we are cut off for our parts.*
(Ezekiel 37:11)

Too many who claim a Christian experience live in plains of plenty - plenty of delusions, plenty of religion, plenty of hypocrisy! The death within is shrouded in a cloak of false spirituality and there is no longer a sense of need (Revelation 3:17-18).

So often, Jesus attacked this falseness in the religious people of His day - the churchgoers, the respectable, those who knew the scriptures but not the Living Word who had spoken them. He declared:-

*Search the scriptures; for in them ye think
ye have eternal life: and they are they
which testify of me.*

*And ye will not come to me, that ye might
have life.*

(John 5:39-40)

> **That is the real problem. We will do anything but come to Him**

That is the real problem. We will do anything but come to Him because we don't want to admit the depravity of our hearts, the darkness within us hates the light.

True worship is born of Spirit and Truth and that is the only basis upon which we can approach Him. Truth demands self-exposure, truth demands an acknowledgment of need, truth demands a casting away of outward forms and an opening of the heart before the only One who can command life.

When He spoke to the scribes and Pharisees, Jesus endorsed the words of Isaiah:-

> *Well hath Esaias prophesied of you*
> *hypocrites, as it is written, This*
> *people honoureth me with their lips,*
> *but their heart is far from me.*
>
> *Howbeit in vain do they worship me,*
> *teaching for doctrines the*
> *commandments of men.*
>
> *(Mark 7:6-7)*

But for those who will admit to the death within, the time for pretence is over. The

The time for pretence is over

bones which Ezekiel viewed could no longer make any claim to life. Similarly, when the body of Lazarus lay in the tomb he had no faith, he had no ability to believe and lay hold of the Word. But there was One outside the tomb who spoke. The One who is the resurrection and the life commanded,

Lazarus, come forth.

(John 11:43)

and his spirit entered into him and he came forth. In a moment it was done.

Can a dead man believe? Can dry bones believe? No, of course not! But when God speaks it happens just because He has spoken,

> *... the words that I speak unto you,*
> *they are spirit, and they are life.*
>
> *(John 6:63)*

He commands life and then it has to be

He commands life and then it has to be. I was once asked to pray for a 22 year old girl who had a medical history of convulsive fits. At the time I was called in she had had a particularly severe attack, had lapsed into a coma, and was due to be hospitalised.

God spoke to me that evening and told me that she would be delivered before midnight. So, I went to the home, talked to the people who were caring for her, and eventually, at about 11.30 pm, we went up to her bedroom.

I can assure you that girl had no faith. She wasn't

But God had promised He would heal her

even aware of what was happening. She was in a deep coma. But God had promised He would heal her.

I rebuked the spirit that bound her and commanded her to be healed in Jesus' name. Immediately she became conscious and sat up, completely normal. Then in His wonderful grace and love, the Lord filled her with His Spirit and I left her rejoicing in all that He had done.

He had gloriously fulfilled His word.

In these days His Spirit has begun to move again. All over the world there's a call to His people to come out of their graves. He speaks and His word is "Live! Live! Live!"

The only ones who can really hear that voice are those who have cried, "Our bones are dried, hope is lost!" But God has come to deal with death; death in any part of your being, death in your body, death in your soul. You're going to come out of your torment, out of your grave, out of your bondages.

For he must reign, till he hath put all enemies under his feet.

The last enemy that shall be destroyed is death.

(1 Corinthians 15:25-26)

Glory to God! There's a Lion of the tribe of Judah who has prevailed over all His enemies! He says, "Live!" His Spirit will begin to flow through you again, until every part is alive with God!

Thus saith the Lord GOD; Come from the four winds, O breath, and breathe upon these slain, that they may live.

(Ezekiel 37:9)

Graves, you're going to open.

Bones, you're going to come together.
Breath, you're going to flow.

Wind, you're going to blow.

God has spoken.

The Almighty Creator has declared it.

God is bringing together an army, a God-birthed army, a God-birthed church, a people who have exchanged their death for His life.

But we had the sentence of death in ourselves, that we should not trust in ourselves, but in God which raiseth the dead;

Who delivered us from so great a death, and doth deliver: in whom we trust that he will yet deliver us;

(2 Corinthians 1:9-10)

AMEN!

Rejoicing in God's goodness.

7

A Contrast In Responses To Jesus

He that rejecteth me, and receiveth not my words, hath one that judgeth him: the word that I have spoken, the same shall judge him in the last day.
(John 12:48)

Two incidents recorded in the New Testament illustrate very different ways of responding to Christ when He comes. Listening to what Jesus actually says is so important in determining our response to Him.

The first of these incidents is found in Matthew 8.

> *And when Jesus was entered into Capernaum, there came unto him a centurion, beseeching him,*

And saying, Lord, my servant lieth at home sick of the palsy, grievously tormented.

And Jesus saith unto him, I will come and heal him.

(Matthew 8:5-7)

Jesus heard of someone suffering and tormented, and He immediately offered to come. That's Jesus, always full of compassion, always ready to meet a need. Love in action!

But notice the centurion's reply.

Lord I am not worthy that thou shouldest come under my roof: but speak the word only, and my servant shall be healed.

(Matthew 8:8)

Who is worthy to have Jesus in his home? The truth is, no one! No one deserves His love, His mercy or His grace.

But that is not the real reason why this man made his excuse. He was afraid to allow Jesus to come too close to his home, his family and his life. He was obviously fond of his servant and he wanted healing for him, but that was all. He shied away from any involvement that might entail a personal commitment, or confrontation!

The centurion acknowledged supernatural power, and being a man of authority himself he also recognised the authority of Christ. But he did not want that authority to impinge on his way of living; he did not want to accept the Saviour as Lord. So he said, "Speak the word only".

> **He shied away from any involvement that might entail a personal commitment, or confrontation!**

Now, it's true that the centurion had faith; Jesus commended him for it. He honestly believed that the word given for his servant would be enough to bring healing. But the Master had said, "I will come" and he replied, "Don't".

That didn't prevent the wonderful Saviour from sending the word to restore the servant to health but Jesus never came to his house. He was kept at a distance, and arm's length.

There are many who understand God's principles. Many have learned that if you have faith in the principles they will operate just as they did for the centurion. God has set laws in both the natural and the spiritual realm and those laws are immutable. But causing laws to operate is very different from openly desiring to know Jesus for Himself.

If Jesus were to say to you "I'm coming to your house, I'm coming to your heart," how would you reply? Would you be one who would answer, "Lord, I'm not ready for You. I'm not worthy. Just speak the word, deliver me, heal me - but please keep away"?

It is significant that shortly after this encounter with the centurion, Jesus went on to declare,

> *The foxes have holes, and the birds of the air have nests; but the Son of man hath not where to lay his head.*
>
> *(Matthew 8:20)*

It was the same throughout His life and ministry. Even at the time of his birth, there was no room for Him in the inn. Very few wanted Him. They wanted what He did, they wanted the miracles, but they didn't want Him for who and what He is.

They wanted what He did, they wanted the miracles, but they didn't want Him. That is how many live today

That is how many live today. A touch, an occasional blessing here and there. God wants us to have so much more! His love, awakened in our hearts, loves Him in return, surrendering everything to Him.

A Contrast In Responses To Jesus

Zacchaeus, in contrast, reacted in the right way when Jesus came:-

> *And, behold, there was a man*
> *named Zacchaeus, which was the chief*
> *among the publicans, and he was rich.*
>
> *And he sought to see Jesus who he was;*
> *and could not for the press, because he*
> *was little of stature.*
>
> *And he ran before, and climbed up*
> *into a sycamore tree to see him: for he*
> *was to pass that way.*
>
> *And when Jesus came to the place, he*
> *looked up, and saw him, and said unto*
> *him, Zacchaeus, make haste, and come*
> *down; for to day I must abide at thy*
> *house.*
>
> *And he made haste, and came down,*
> *and received him joyfully.*
>
> *(Luke 19:2-6)*

Notice the response of Zacchaeus in comparison to that of the centurion. Jesus said to each of them, "I'm coming to your home". One replied, "Oh, please don't bother, I only need healing for my servant"; the other made haste to welcome the Saviour.

85

Of course all the onlookers murmured against the Lord when they realised he was going to visit the home of a publican. As far as they were concerned Zacchaeus was to be avoided. They could find a hundred things wrong with him and a thousand reasons why Jesus shouldn't have anything to do with him. They couldn't see that this man had a needy heart and that he was prepared to open it to the Saviour.

> **This man had a needy heart and was prepared to open it**

Jesus paid no attention to their criticisms. He didn't care at all. His heart is for the lost! He comes to save those who, in the world's terms, should never be saved.

Isn't it wonderful how God chooses the offscourings of the earth, the vile and the filthy to be part of his glorious kingdom of grace!

But God hath chosen the foolish things of the world to confound the wise; and God hath chosen the weak things of the world to confound the things which are mighty.

And base things of the world, and things which are despised, hath God chosen, yea,

and things which are not, to bring to
nought things that are.

That no flesh should glory in his presence
(1 Corinthians 1:27-29)

When Jesus comes, what is your response? Is it to say, "I'm not worthy", or is it to welcome the Saviour into your heart?

Of course the wrongs are going to be sorted out and put right. Look at what happened to Zacchaeus. It wasn't long before he admitted that he had acquired much of his wealth by cheating and malpractice and he set himself to make restitution.

Behold, Lord, the half of my goods I give
to the poor; and if I have taken anything
from any man by false accusation, I
restore him fourfold.

(Luke 19:8)

Then came that wonderful declaration of Jesus,

This day is salvation come to this
house, forsomuch as he also is a
son of Abraham.

(Luke 19:9)

Zacchaeus had been birthed into the great household of faith.

Jesus didn't wait until the man's life was right. He didn't wait until he had attained some tremendous

Jesus didn't wait until the man's life was right

spiritual height. The truth is that God will bless us when we're all wrong, and in blessing us, He'll cause us to turn and become right!

For it is God which worketh in you both
to will and to do of his good pleasure.
(Philippians 2:13)

That is the secret. It is His love and grace which reaches out. His faith can transform that which seems to be 'untransformable'! All we have to do is to open our hearts to His coming. He does the rest!

Zacchaeus didn't approach the Lord with a long list of demands. He had heard so much about this Jesus that he just wanted to see Him for himself. He didn't foresee that Jesus would call him down from the tree and out of the circumstances of his life. He didn't realise that the encounter would revolutionise his whole way of living and bring glory to his heart. In fact, Zacchaeus didn't do anything except receive the One who does it all!

What, then, was the difference between the centurion and the publican? They were two men who met with the Saviour; two men to whom the Lord made a similar offer. The one was content with a miracle, the other welcomed the King who works the miracles.

> *When Jesus comes the tempter's power is broken*
> *When Jesus comes the tears are wiped away*
> *He takes the gloom and fills the life with glory*
> *For all is changed when Jesus comes to stay.*

When we come to Jesus He meets every need - the needs of children, the needs of adults, the whole family.

8

My Son Shall Live

Jesus said... I am the resurrection, and the life: he that believeth in me, though he were dead, yet shall he live.
(John 11:25)

Many Christians have such a puny understanding of the power contained within the words which God speaks. In the beginning, it was His Word which spoke creation into existence and that Word has never failed. As the scripture teaches in Hebrews, He upholds

... all things by the word of his power
(Hebrews 1:3)

I could never believe in the Biblical account of Creation until God birthed me from above. The natural mind is carnal and at enmity with God, but a true birth brings reality. When I came into life I

> ### The truth is that every word which God speaks will come to pass

found it impossible not to believe in the creation story because I had a relationship with the Creator God. I believed Him and so I believed His word.

The truth is that every word which God speaks will come to pass.

For as the rain cometh down, and the snow from heaven, and returneth not thither, but watereth the earth, and maketh it bring forth and bud, that it may give seed to the sower, and bread to the eater:

So shall my word be that goeth forth out of my mouth: it shall not return unto me void, but it shall accomplish that which I please, and it shall prosper in the thing whereto I sent it.

(Isaiah 55:10-11)

Let us look at an account of a woman in the Old Testament who learned how to lay hold of the word which God had given her, even when all the natural circumstances of her life seemed to deny it.

And it fell on a day, that Elisha passed
to Shunem, where was a great woman;
and she constrained him to eat bread.
And so it was, that as oft as he passed
by, he turned in thither to eat bread.

And she said unto her husband, Behold
now, I perceive that this is an holy
man of God, which passeth by us
continually.

Let us make a little chamber, I pray
thee, on the wall; and let us set for him
there a bed, and a table, and a stool,
and a candlestick: and it shall be,
when he cometh to us, that he shall
turn in thither.

(2 Kings 4:8-10)

Whether this woman was first motivated by
curiosity, compassion or some strange inner
compulsion the Scriptures do not tell us. What they
do reveal is that she was a great woman and she
"constrained" Elisha to visit her home. She was not
going to take "No" for an answer!

So it became a custom that whenever the prophet
was travelling that way he would have a meal with
the couple. They must have shared concerning the
truths of God, for the woman soon recognised that

this man was different, he was one who knew God. A spiritual hunger stirred in her heart and she persuaded her husband to let her prepare a room for Elisha so that he could spend more time with them.

> **For some, intermittent encounter is all they desire**

Many people attend church services and their only concern is to receive some blessing from God. That is sufficient. Afterwards, they're quite content to return to their own life, their own business, their own ways. An intermittent encounter is all they desire and therefore all they receive.

Nonetheless, there are others for whom that is not enough. It is not enough for the Lord to come and just break bread with them; it is not enough for Him to spend some time with them occasionally. Within the heart is a deep longing to make a place for Him to come and lodge; a place of abiding; a place of rest.

The Holy Spirit searches for such places for Jesus to abide in. As Noah sent forth the dove to seek out dry land so God has sent forth His Spirit to seek out hearts that will be resting places for Him. The Holy Spirit will pass by continually, even as Elisha did, until that time when the heart is ready to say, "I've made a place for You to dwell."

> *And it fell on a day, that he came thither,*
> *and he turned into the chamber, and lay*
> *there.*
>
> *(2 Kings 4:11)*

The prophet had come to stay! Then everything began to change! Whilst he rested in the little room she had prepared for him, Elisha's heart was moved to find a way to repay the woman for her kindness.

She was not an ambitious person; she did not come with any demands even when Gehazi, Elisha's servant, gave her the opportunity to do so. But Gehazi perceived the one great void in her life - she had no child. Accordingly, she was called to Elisha's room and he spoke the wonderful words of God's promise to her.

> *About this season, according to the time*
> *of life, thou shalt embrace a son. And she*
> *said, Nay, my lord, thou man of God,*
> *do not lie unto thine handmaid.*
>
> *(2 Kings 4:16)*

A child, a son! - she couldn't believe it! She knew this was a man of God! Could it be that he would lie to her? Could it be that after all the years of barren waiting, her reproach would at last be taken away?

It was a word sovereignly given by God. The woman had abandoned hope.

God had spoken to her heart

Perhaps she had been too afraid to ask in case her request was rejected. But now in her simple way she took that word and she believed that it would be, because God had spoken to her heart by His prophet.

We all know the story of how the promise was fulfilled and a little boy was born into the home of this Shunammite couple. However, in the midst of their happiness there remained a further test of faith, for the child suddenly fell ill and died.

To the average person it would have seemed that the promise had been in vain. But this woman was not average! As we consider her reactions to the tragedy it becomes clear why she is described in the Scriptures as a great woman.

Years before she had made a place in her heart and in her home for Elisha. So now, at this time of crisis, she went straight to that place. She lifted the child and took him to the room of the man of God, laying the little lifeless body gently on the bed.

You know, if you have truly made a place for God in your life, if you are one who has developed a relationship with Him, you can always come into the place of fellowship. Whatever happens, whatever the circumstances, you can come to Him and know that there will be an answer.

The eyes of faith look beyond the natural realm with all its problems

Fixed upon the One who cannot fail

and impossibilities and are fixed upon the One who cannot fail, the One whose name is Love.

Having laid her son to rest in the place from where she had received the promise, the woman went in search of the man of God. She knew he would have the answer. She wouldn't listen to her husband's objections; she brushed aside Gehazi's questions, for she realised he could do nothing to help her. She went straight to Elisha, catching hold of his feet as if she would never let him go. Nothing was going to keep her from the one who had spoken the promise. Gehazi tried to push her away but Elisha saw her distress and intervened;

> *Then she said, Did I desire a son of my*
> *lord? did I not say, Do not deceive me?*
> *(2 Kings 4:28)*

Do you see what she did? She went right back to the original word, reminding Elisha that she had never demanded the child, he had been given as a son of promise. At the time she had begged the prophet not to deceive her, and she believed that even now he would honour that request.

Somehow, this simple woman had grasped a secret. Her trust was in the Giver, not in the gift. Even tragedy could not shake that trust. She knew the birth of the boy had been nothing to do with her faith. God had given her a son and she intended to keep him. Death was irrelevant, for death had no power to extinguish the word.

> **Her trust was in the Giver, not in the gift. Even tragedy could not shake that trust**

... The grass withereth, and the flower thereof falleth away:
But the word of the Lord endureth for ever ...

(1 Peter 1:24-25)

Very often, when God speaks a word to us we take it so lightly, we forget so easily. When circumstances seem to contradict it, we believe the circumstances rather than the living word of the living God. Disaster strikes and we abandon faith in the word that was given to us, the sure promise.

But this Shunammite woman maintained faith. Over the course of time she had developed a relationship with the man of God which caused her to trust his word. Now in her trouble she sought out Elisha and she had no intention of letting him go until her child was restored. Even when Gehazi was sent to deal with the situation her response to his master was clear.

> *... As the Lord liveth, and as thy soul liveth, I will not leave thee ...*
> *(2 Kings 4:30)*

She knew the servant did not have the answer; she was staying with Elisha.

When the prophet saw the tenacity of her faith, he agreed to go with her. Gehazi's mission had been unsuccessful so Elisha went up to the little room where the lifeless body lay and shutting everyone else out he sought God. He believed the word that had been spoken in that very place so long ago, he had seen the woman's great faith and above all he knew His God. There had to be an answer! And there was!

Before long life stirred again in that young boy.

*And he called Gehazi, and said, Call
this Shunammite. So he called her. And
when she was come in unto him, he said,
Take up thy son.*

*Then she went in, and fell at his feet,
and bowed herself to the ground, and took
up her son, and went out.*

(2 Kings 4:36-37)

> **You know, you can
> return to any word
> which God speaks to
> you, again and again
> and again**

What a faith! What an answer!

You know, you can return to any word of promise which God speaks to you, again and again and again. The circumstances are irrelevant, the impossibilities don't matter at all because within each and every promise spoken by the Creator God is the power for an eternal work.

A woman of lesser faith might have been defeated by the tragic death of her child. But not this Shunammite mother. She could not accept that Elisha would deceive her, that the gift so wonderfully given had been snatched away for ever. Within herself she said:-

"No, the word worked for yesterday and it will yet

work for today. He promised me a son and a son I shall keep. Death has no rights!"

> **The word worked for yesterday and it will yet work for today!!**

Then she acted it out. That is true faith. Like Abraham she was prepared to cling on to the promise of God no matter what!

But wilt thou know, O vain man, that faith without works is dead?

Was not Abraham our father justified by works, when he had offered Isaac his son upon the altar?

Seest thou how faith wrought with his works, and by works was faith made perfect?

(James 2:20-22)

Have you got the same faith as the Shunammite woman? Have you, like her, made room for God in your life? Has He spoken to you? Has He done things within you but somehow you've lost the glory of them? Have you just let them go? If so, you can come right back to His feet, you can lay hold of Him. He cannot deny His name and He cannot deny His word and He will fulfill His promises without fail.

> *For all the promises of God in him*
> *are yea, and in him Amen, unto the*
> *glory of God by us.*
>
> *(2 Corinthians 1:20)*

That's where each and every promise is fulfilled - in the person of Jesus Christ. Our faith must be in Him. Then His faith operates to bring about the impossible.

> **The only thing which prevents you receiving is you don't ask.**

He says that if you ask you will receive. The only thing which prevents you is that you don't ask. Did He not say that He would heal you? Did He not say that He would forgive, cleanse, release? Why then the sickness, the guilt, the bondages?

Come to Him with that cry of faith in your heart - "O God, fulfil your word. I have a right to it because you spoke it to me. It is eternal and it shall be! I will not let it go!!"

> *Cast not away therefore your*
> *confidence, which hath great*
> *recompence of reward.*

For ye have need of patience, that,
after ye have done the will of God,
ye might receive the promise.

(Hebrews 10:35-36)

Bill Ennis, up and running after being healed of chronic pain from shattered vertebrae in his lower back.

9

What God Says Happens

God is not a man, that he should lie;
neither the son of man, that he should
repent: hath he said, and shall he not do
it? or hath he spoken, and shall he not
make it good?
(Numbers 23:19)

When God speaks a word it has to be. Sometimes we find the circumstances seem to say it's impossible, it cannot be! But when God speaks it's impossible for it not to be!

He's able to reach in and meet the deepest need of any life, whether physical or spiritual. That's the wonder of it all - what God says always happens!

In Genesis 46 there is an interesting account of God speaking to Jacob when he and his family were on their way to Egypt to be reunited with Joseph. God's words held a promise:-

> *I am God, the God of thy father: fear not to go down into Egypt; for I will there make of thee a great nation:*
>
> *I will go down with thee into Egypt; and I will also surely bring thee up again:*
> *(Genesis 46:3-4)*

God spoke that word but He never told Jacob how He would bring it to pass. That was hidden, but the promise was sure.

He never told him of the days after Joseph's death when another Pharaoh would arise. He never explained how the children of Israel would suffer in that land; how they would be enslaved and scourged by merciless taskmasters; how their baby sons would be torn from them to be put to death by the cruel edict of a dictator king.

He tells us what He'll do, not how He'll do it

God has His secrets. Thank God He keeps them secret!!! He tells us what He'll do, not how He'll do it.

He knows how easily our hearts become afraid, how easily we fall into despair and so He doesn't always explain that the pathway will sometimes take us through trials and pain. Of course, when God speaks the word of promise, we're so thrilled, so full of faith and anticipation that we expect it to happen tomorrow, if not sooner!

Jacob, by faith, took God at His word and went down to Egypt. He believed God even as his grandfather Abraham had done. He didn't foresee what his obedience would entail. Four hundred long years were to elapse before the promise was fulfilled. Four hundred years' wait. Jacob had died and been laid to rest in the land of his fathers before the appointed day dawned. But God kept His word. He made of Jacob a great nation, according to His promise.

... for I will hasten my word to perform it.
(Jeremiah 1:12)

God always keeps His word. Don't ever lose heart because everything seems to be going wrong. God knows from the beginning what lies ahead. We just have to learn to rest in this God. What He wants us to know He'll tell us. As day follows day, all will be revealed. Each day we'll find sufficient grace to cope with whatever we have to go through. We won't have the grace before the trial, but when the need arises we'll find it there.

Nothing God brings into our lives is for our destruction. It's for our benefit

Nothing God brings into our lives is for our destruction. It's for our benefit. Sometimes He leads us in ways that are beyond our understanding. But His purpose is one of love - to bring us into life, to prepare us for glory.

Remember how Jesus dealt with the family of Lazarus at the time of his illness and death.

Now a certain man was sick, named Lazarus, of Bethany, the town of Mary and her sister Martha.

Therefore his sisters sent unto him, saying, Lord, behold, he whom thou lovest is sick.

When Jesus heard that, he said, This sickness is not unto death, but for the glory of God, that the Son of God might be glorified thereby.

Now Jesus loved Martha, and her sister, and Lazarus.

When he had heard therefore that he was sick, he abode two days still in the same place where he was.

(John 11:1, 3-6)

Jesus loved them, but at the hour of their need He appeared to have totally ignored them. He deliberately delayed going to Bethany. That seems a very strange thing for the Lord to have done. In fact, Lazarus had already been buried four days by the time that Jesus arrived. The family was torn with grief and regrets that for some reason the Master had not arrived in time. True love is prepared to let suffering happen that we might learn the deeper lessons of faith.

Martha, impetuous, outspoken and busy Martha, came running out to greet the Lord with these words:-

> *Lord, if thou hadst been here, my brother had not died.*
>
> *But I know, that even now, whatsoever thou wilt ask of God, God will give it thee.*
>
> *Jesus saith unto her, Thy brother shall rise again.*
>
> *Martha saith unto him, I know that he shall rise again in the resurrection at the last day.*
>
> *(John 11:21-24)*

Martha had all the theory right. Her doctrine was sound. But somehow the faith to accept that Jesus would raise her beloved brother from death immediately was beyond her grasp. As soon as the Lord said, "Your brother's going to rise again," it was as if her confidence evaporated. It was impossible! Lazarus was dead and buried! She could believe for a resurrection at the last day but not for today.

Jesus said unto her, I am the resurrection, and the life: he that believeth in me, though he were dead, yet shall he live:

And whosoever liveth and believeth in me shall never die. Believest thou this?

(John 11:25-26)

He did not condemn

He did not condemn Martha; He understood her fear and confusion. He simply said, "Martha, do you believe I am the resurrection? I am the life. I am. Do you believe it?"

Again, Martha's response was so correct.

She saith unto him, Yea, Lord: I believe that thou art the Christ, the Son of God, which should come into the world.

> *And when she had so said, she went her*
> *way, and called Mary her sister*
> *secretly, saying, The Master is come,*
> *and calleth for thee.*
>
> *(John 11:27-28)*

Martha had had enough! She'd been faced up with questions which were beyond her. She couldn't cope with them any more. She thought it was time to shift some of the responsibility to her sister.

> *Then when Mary was come where Jesus*
> *was, and saw him, she fell down at his*
> *feet, saying unto him, Lord, if thou hadst*
> *been here, my brother had not died.*
>
> *(John 11:32)*

Mary was just like Martha!

We say"if only" so often. It's a way of thought which is really a cover-up for all that deep-rooted unbelief in our hearts. If only God had intervened at this point, or at that point we could have been helped. But now it's too late. It's gone too far. There's no hope now!!

No one believed that Jesus was going to raise Lazarus from the dead. The Jews who were with the two sisters voiced the same regrets - if only Jesus had come sooner, perhaps He could have prevented the tragedy. Now all they had to do was show Him the grave. It was too late.

> **There was only One who had faith**

There was only One who had faith on that day - Jesus Himself. He called for the stone to be removed from the entrance to the tomb and immediately Martha objected.

> *Lord, by this time he stinketh: for he hath been dead four days.*
>
> *(John 11:39)*

We're just the same! In our lives we take Jesus to the graves within. We take Him to view those problems, which we've buried beneath the boulders of hopelessness and erected a neat little sign - Rest in Peace! It is too late for changes now!

Then He speaks those wonderful words, "Take ye away the stone" - and we become defensive. We don't want our inner heart to be exposed. We don't want anyone to see the death and corruption that works within.

We are quite prepared to believe that one day those twisted parts of our nature will be transformed. But on this day, at this time we don't want Christ to deal with us. It will happen in the twinkling of an eye on the last day when the trumpet sounds. Not now?

But Jesus broke through Martha's fears, pointing her to the glory which is the reward of faith in Him.

> *Said I not unto thee, that, if thou wouldest believe, thou shouldest see the glory of God?*
>
> *(John 11:40)*

What then was the secret? What was Martha to believe?

Jesus had already given her the answer when she came out to meet Him.

> *I am the resurrection, and the life: he that believeth in me, though he were dead, yet shall he live.*
>
> *(John 11:25)*

In other words, "Martha, don't struggle to believe for a miracle. Just believe that I am the resurrection, I am the life. Believe in Me."

That is how we receive healing, salvation, deliverance or whatever else it is we need. It's belief in the Living Christ. That's what brings reality into a heart. It's not my faith, it's His! His promises are true!

> **That's what brings reality into a heart. It's not my faith, it's His!**

There is no place in

our lives where Jesus cannot come. He can transform the stench of death into the sweetness of His life. We don't have to hide behind those words of unbelief,

"If only Jesus had been here!"

For four hundred years the children of Israel sweated and toiled after the death of Joseph. The persecutions and afflictions were great. But God had made a promise to Jacob, "I'm going to make you a great nation."

In spite of the adversity, Jacob's descendants multiplied and grew. Yet they cried, "Where is our God, the God of our fathers?" The truth is, He was there all the time, waiting only for the fullness of time to come when His glory would be revealed. He is always there, because He loves us.

Jesus will call you out with that voice of life

There are no graveclothes which can hide your innermost sin from Him. There is no tomb that can keep you from His love and power. There is no rock heavy enough to hold the soul in death when the Lord of Glory comes and speaks the word of release. Jesus will call you out with that voice of life,

"You thought it was hopeless. You thought there was no solution. Today is your day. Today I've come to speak life into the depths of your being. Though ye were dead, yet shall ye live."

Praying for a sick child brought to a Music and Miracles service at Peniel Church

10

Faith In Him

Paul, a servant of God, and an apostle
of Jesus Christ, according to the faith of
God's elect, and the acknowledging of
the truth which is after godliness;
In hope of eternal life, which God,
that cannot lie, promised before
the world began;
(Titus 1:1-2)

All true faith is really based in the belief, the certainty, that God cannot lie.

He made an eternal promise before the foundation of the world that He would bring many sons unto Glory! For this purpose He sent His Son into the world, to redeem those whom He calls.

All God has promised He will perform

The gospel is so simple, so sure, because it is based on the Covenant Word of our unchangeable God. The fact is that all God has promised He will perform. He promised that there would be healing, cleansing, forgiveness, deliverance and He hasn't changed His mind! He never will! He initiated the whole plan of salvation and He will also bring it to completion.

> *For we ourselves also were sometimes foolish, disobedient, deceived, serving divers lust and pleasures, ...*
>
> *But after that the kindness and love of God our Saviour toward man appeared, Not by works of righteousness which we have done, but according to his mercy he saved us, by the washing of regeneration, and receiving of the Holy Ghost;*
>
> *(Titus 3:3-5)*

Salvation is neither conditional upon our set beliefs, nor our responses. It is all according to His wonderful mercy and grace. Any time a man receives something from God, it is because God has graciously bestowed it upon him as a gift, undeserved and unconditional.

After the resurrection Jesus appeared to His disciples and instructed them to remain at Jerusalem to await the promise of the Father. I'm sure they didn't know what to expect, and that they didn't expect what they received! They heard the sound of a mighty, rushing wind, flames of fire appeared above their heads and they were gloriously filled with the Holy Ghost and spoke in tongues. God had fulfilled His promise and baptised them in the Holy Spirit. Jesus Christ fulfilled His Promise when He sent forth His Spirit, poured out on all flesh on the day of Pentecost. It is still His gracious provision for all His people in this day.

- Salvation is all His work, and His alone.
- Who does the saving? Jesus.
- Who is our justification? Jesus.
- Who is our sanctification? Jesus.
- Who heals, delivers, sets free? Jesus.

I haven't got faith in myself and I haven't got faith in my theories, because neither is effectual. I have faith in Him!

Abraham, the great patriarch of faith, believed God for Himself, not just for the promises He gave. He was prepared to sacrifice his only son, Isaac, the child of promise, the seed through whom God had covenanted to establish a people, because He believed His God.

He knew that the One who had given the child of promise was also able to raise him up from death. So often, we strive and struggle to work up faith, to believe for this or that. Often preachers say "just believe for healing," but that is the last thing we are able to do. We struggle to believe because we need help, but we are trying to believe ourselves into an experience. What happens? The doubts still gnaw inside, the questions and fears bombard our minds. Even when we try to believe with all our might, we can't. The attempt is a miserable failure.

But God doesn't demand that of us! He is only too aware of our frailties! He knows that of ourselves we have no faith and can do nothing.

> The Shepherd does not ask of thee
> Faith in thy faith, but only faith in Him
> And this He meant in saying 'Come to Me'
> In light or darkness, seek to do His will
> And leave the work of faith to Jesus still
>
> (Anon)

Not faith in your healing, but Faith in Him

It's so simple! Not faith in your faith, your healing, your deliverance, but Faith in Him.

His faith is the vehicle by which the promises of God

became a living reality within us. Faith is His work. Have faith in God.

> *... faith cometh by hearing, and hearing by the word of God.*
>
> *(Romans 10:17)*

He does the work by His faith

All we have to do is to come to Him, knowing that He is who and what He says He is. That is all God requires. He is the One who works everything out. He is our Redeemer, Saviour, Healer, Restorer and Mighty Deliverer. He does the work.

> *In whom also we have obtained an inheritance, being predestinated according to the purpose of Him who worketh all things after the counsel of His own will.*
>
> *(Ephesians 1:11)*

The gospel is not an exposition of the `maybe': maybe one day I'll muster sufficient faith to believe, maybe one day God will meet with me. It's a message of grace from a God who has already purposed to redeem, to deliver, to set us free. That's why He is called the Saviour, the Redeemer, the Mighty God. Long before our birth He prepared the way of salvation for us. Time and time again when Jesus was on earth He was moved with compassion when He saw the needs of the multitude. He never turned anyone away. He invited all to come to Him and met all their needs. That invitation to "COME" still stands. He hasn't changed.

In Matthew 9 we find the story of the two blind men who followed Jesus, crying out for mercy. He said to them:-

> *Believe ye that I am able to do this?*
> *(Matthew 9:28)*

That was all He asked - just one question, "Do you believe I'm able to do this?"

That is all He would ask you - "Do you believe Me? I can come into the midst of the storm in your heart to still it. I can rebuke all types of disease and sickness. I can deal with the deep inward groanings, the pain within. I can speak a word of life into a dead soul and that soul shall live. Do you believe Me? Do you believe that I can do this for you now?"

He can do all things. It takes but a word, a touch of His hand. Come simply to Him, He will do it!

You say that you've already asked. Well,

keep on asking. You say that you've knocked: keep knocking. You think He doesn't care, but He does. That same compassion still reaches out today. He hears, He answers, He can do all things. It takes but a word, a touch of His hand. Come simply to Him, He will do it!

> *God is not a man, that he should lie:*
> *neither the son of man, that he should*
> *repent: hath he said, and shall he not*
> *do it? or hath he spoken, and shall*
> *he not make it good?*
>
> *(Numbers 23:19)*

He replied to the blind men:-

> *According to your faith be it unto you.*
> *(Matthew 9:29)*

They had faith in His ability to open their eyes, and put their trust in Him.

Mercy, healing, deliverance are this day available for you. Even now the wonderful Saviour intercedes before the throne of the Father on your behalf.

*But the righteousness which is of
faith speaketh on this wise, Say not in
thine heart, Who shall ascend into
heaven? (that is, to bring Christ down
from above:)*

*Or, Who shall descend into the deep?
(that is, to bring up Christ again from
the dead.)*

*But what saith it? The word is nigh thee,
even in thy mouth, and in thy heart:
that is, the word of faith which we preach;*

*That if thou shalt confess with thy mouth
the Lord Jesus, and shalt believe in thine
heart that God hath raised him from
the dead, thou shalt be saved.*

*For with the heart man believeth unto
righteousness; and with the mouth
confession is made unto salvation.*

(Romans 10:6-10)

> **The word of
> faith confesses
> Christ and His
> resurrection
> power**

We are called to confess Jesus and believe in His resurrection, not to confess ourselves into an experience. The word of faith confesses Christ and His resurrection power.

Jesus Christ is the answer. He is ready to be your very life, your Saviour, Redeemer, justifier, sanctifier, healer and deliverer and everything you need right NOW!!

Jesus is "the author and finisher of our Faith!"

Jonathan Cope had pancreatitis - eighty percent of his pancreas had ceased to function, and there was a very real possibility that his pancreas and other organs might be permanently damaged. There was also a very real possibility that he might not survive at all.
Bishop Reid prayed for him in hospital and by the following morning, Jonathan was a new person - bright and in a stable condition.

11

A Matter Of Life And Death

Jonathan Cope

For accountant Jonathan Cope, life suddenly stopped adding up early in 1995, when he was struck down by the killer disease pancreatitis.

"For years I had been a confirmed atheist" he told Peniel. "My wife was a Christian, but I found church tedious, and I only went for special occasions like weddings. I preferred to rely on myself rather than some mystical external force, and I thought I had everything sewn up very nicely, thank you. It was my life, and I was in control."

That Jonathan was not in control was brought home with a vengeance in May 1995.

"I developed very severe stomach pains, and was rushed into hospital. Suddenly life didn't look so secure after all." The prognosis was very poor. I had pancreatitis - eighty percent of my pancreas had ceased to function, and there was a very real possibility that my pancreas and other organs might be permanently damaged. There was also a very real possibility that I might not survive at all."

Balanced between life and death, Jonathan suddenly found the need to do some serious thinking.

"Things looked very black," he told us. "When you're in that sort of situation, you begin to think about where you're heading. I realised as I lay in hospital that I needed to change my life and start to rely upon God. I knew I hadn't been living right, and I knew that I needed to turn to someone else. Self-reliance wasn't an option any more."

"There was really only one place I could turn. My wife, son and daughter had been regular members of the congregation at Peniel for many years, and although I had seldom set foot inside the place myself, I asked if Bishop Reid could come and pray for me. His message to me, when he arrived, was very direct - you'd better fight for life, because if you die, you certainly aren't going to heaven. Then he prayed - just a very brief prayer and left."

A quick prayer was all it took, however. Dr Joseph Mathai, who was treating Jonathan at the time, takes up the story.

"Jonathan's case notes put him in the category of 'grievous risk to health and life'. It looked as though surgery was going to be essential. At the time Jonathan was prayed for, he was critically ill. But by the following morning, he was a new person - bright and in a stable condition."

Recovery from pancreatitis is not unknown, as Dr Mathai explained. "Patients do recover," he told us, "but over a period of time. In Jonathan's case, the improvement occurred so rapidly we must conclude that something other than the treatment and Jonathan's own resources intervened to bring about the change."

Some five years later, Jonathan is perfectly fit and well, with no trace of pancreatitis. Since his recovery, he has been baptised and is now a regular member of the Peniel congregation, revelling in coming to know more closely the God who plucked him back from the brink of death.

David Gregg, lying on the floor during a service at Peniel Church, suffering from chronic sciatica.
When Bishop Reid prayed for him everything changed.
By the end of the meeting he was back to normal,
perfectly able to walk on his own. One hundred per cent
fit again, he's now back at work full time.

David Gregg says, "If you don't call this a miracle, I don't know what you'd call it!"

12

The Lame Shall Walk

David Gregg

9.55 am, and last minute arrivals for Peniel's Sunday morning service are gingerly stepping around the figure of a man lying on the floor, in evident distress...

Five minutes ago, he was half carried, half dragged into the hall, arms draped over the shoulders of two friends. They laid him gently on the floor and he has not moved since.

In two hours time, he will stand up unaided.

Then within a couple of minutes, he will begin to walk.

At the end of the meeting he will stride out of the hall under his own steam, completely healed by Jesus and outpacing the friends who brought him in.

Peniel has been privileged to witness some amazing miracles over recent years. Yet even for a congregation which has been present at all of these, the events of one Sunday morning some three years ago have made a deep and lasting impression.

For two years, Maldon resident David Gregg lived in a torment of agonising back pain. Diagnosed as suffering from sciatica, David was prescribed pain-killers and rest - something which, being self-employed, he could ill afford.

The treatment did little to help. Nor did osteopathy, nor physiotherapy. David's condition continued to worsen, and at last he was admitted to Basildon hospital for further investigation. Any hope that this might finally lead to effective treatment was soon dashed, however; tests revealed nothing new, and his physical decline continued.

Walking and sleeping were absolute agony

Before long walking - and even sleeping - were absolute agony, and the driving and heavy moving involved in David's job as a washing machine repair man were rapidly becoming more than he could cope with. He was less and less able to work, and the family's income was rapidly drying up. Financial ruin was becoming a real possibility.

Despite this, however, it was the business which was to provide David with his first step back towards health, for a friend called to ask if he could fix his washing machine, and hearing of David's predicament, invited him along to a Brentwood church where he felt sure he could be healed - and just so there could be no possible doubt, he lent him a video showing other miraculous healings at Peniel.

It was perhaps still touch and go whether David would make it. The night before the service, the pain in his leg became so bad that he had to call out the emergency doctor, who, unable to prescribe anything more effective himself, had given him a letter to his own GP recommending stronger pain killers. Of the journey to Peniel David remembers nothing - apart, that is, from being in absolute agony. He needed to be carried into the hall, and could do no more than collapse on to the floor, still in such overwhelming pain that he was all but oblivious of the events around him.

"I can't recall anything about the meeting up to the point where Bishop Reid prayed for me," David told us, "but when he did pray, everything changed. He told me to stand and to start walking up and down the hall. It seemed ridiculous - an impossibility - but as I did so, suddenly the pain began to drain out of me. By the end of the meeting I was back to normal, perfectly able to walk on my own with no problems at all."

"Since then, I haven't looked back," David continued, "and I've never taken a pain killer since that day!"

I've never taken a pain killer since that day!

"I'm one hundred per cent fit again, I'm in the middle of opening a shop in Maldon, and I have all the work I can handle, which means I'm able to get back on my feet financially as well as physically."

"After I was healed, I suppose you could best sum up the reaction of my family and friends as a mixture of astonishment and scepticism. But one things for sure - they can't deny the evidence of their own eyes!"

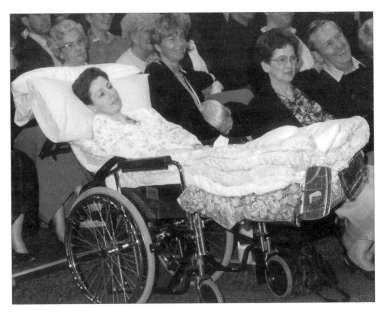

Amanda Bucket, who suffered from ME for 18 years, bedridden for 10 of those years, has seen dramatic and continued improvement in her condition since being prayed for at Peniel.

13

Shocked And Amazed!

Amanda Bucket

S hocked and amazed. That was how ME victim Amanda Bucket described her GP's reaction to the transformation in her physical well-being since she went for prayer at Peniel Pentecostal Church five years ago.

ME victim's transformation amazes GP

A victim of glandular fever at school, Amanda never fully recovered, and although she managed to complete her education and start training as a nurse, she was forced to give up after twelve months in the face of deteriorating health.

Now in her late thirties, Amanda had suffered from ME for eighteen years, although it was eight years before the disease was diagnosed as such. Some ten years ago, her condition worsened to the point where doctors believed she would die.

> **Too weak to live**

"At that time, they transferred me to a clinic, where I spent the next two and a half years," she told us. "My whole body was limp, just like a jelly. I felt as though I was too weak even to carry on living. It was all just too much."

"At the clinic I had the best treatments there were going... and at the end of it all, they had to admit defeat. I returned home no better than when I'd left."

In desperation, Amanda and her family turned to alternative therapies. "I tried reflexology, acupuncture, natural medicines... you name it, I had it," Amanda recalls. "We spent thousands and thousands - and still it made no difference."

"Then my mother happened to get hold of a copy of Trumpet Call, Peniel's newspaper, and suggested we should come down to Peniel. By that time, I'd been bed-bound for about ten years. To give you an idea of the state I was in, I could just about pick up grapes and use a baby feeder. Anything else had to be done for me - and I mean anything. Even something as simple as having a wash was beyond me."

"As you can imagine, the journey was quite an undertaking - and by the time I got to Peniel, I was worse than ever. I couldn't even manage to sit through the meeting. I remember having to lie in a bed at the front of the church, limp and all but lifeless."

The improvement was remarkable

The improvement, when it came, was remarkable. Following prayer - and much to the amazement of Amanda's carer who had nursed her over a four year period - Amanda began to respond in a new way to her daily massages and exercise regime. Movements which had previously been impossible were suddenly within her grasp, and she quickly grew stronger.

Three months later, Amanda and her mother, Nora, were back at Peniel for further prayer. This time, with a little help, she was able to walk eight steps - a considerable feat for a person who, for years, had been all but unable to stand up.

The improvement had not gone unnoticed by Amanda's GP. "When he came to visit," Amanda told us, "he asked whether perhaps I'd been keeping a twin sister under the bed and had swapped places with her. He just couldn't get over the difference in me. He's not a believer, but he was ready to admit that whatever it was that had happened, he couldn't take any credit for it."

Amanda is gradually getting stronger, and is looking forward to the complete return of her health and strength.

"I can see a friend every day; it is so good to be able to talk with people and hug people again. I also speak on the phone to friends every day, which is a real joy. I can prepare myself snacks, as well as feed and bathe myself."

"One big delight is to see the sky, trees, birds and insects and to feel the breeze on my face. I've been for a wheelchair walk in the woods several times - something I've been yearning to do for years - and took my 8 year old dog for our first walk together."

"My nieces came to visit me recently too, and they were so overwhelmed when I came walking out of my room to meet them that they burst into tears. God has done something very wonderful for me."

*Katie Medland, diagnosed with psoriatic arthritis,
had such pain and stiffness in her joints that
everyday tasks and sports became almost impossible.
After prayer, she was soon back on the hockey pitch,
fully recovered and living a normal life.*

14

Katie Grasps The Future

Katie Medland

As a normal, healthy teenager, Katie Medland's future looked bright. She was doing well academically, enjoyed sport, and had helped her school to the finals of the English Schools Under 16 table tennis competition. Then, all of a sudden, Katie's world began to fall apart...

"Things started going wrong just after my GCSEs. I was looking forward to some well-earned rest when suddenly I started to feel stiff."

"At first I didn't think much about it, assuming it would get better of its own accord, but it didn't. Before long I could hardly walk, and the doctor diagnosed arthritis."

"Initially, anti-inflammatory drugs brought a dramatic improvement, but the effects soon wore off, and before long I was worse than ever. My joints were so painful that it was all I could do to get out of bed. Sometimes my fingers just locked up completely, and I had to have them massaged for ages before I could use them. Once it took 20 minutes to open a tin."

The strain was taking its toll on Katie's mum, Lynn, too.

"We tried putting Katie on a special diet. It was terrible - no red meat, no wheat, no dairy products, no citrus fruits. Still Katie got no better."

"We were even beginning to think about pricing wheelchairs. I was in a dreadful state. Some nights I used to cry myself to sleep."

The worst time of all was the day that Katie's GCSE results came through. She'd done brilliantly - but that same day we heard from Katie's consultant that she'd reached a definite diagnosis - Katie had psoriatic arthritis. We were devastated."

"At the next church service, Katie put in a request for prayer. For several weeks nothing seemed to change, and then one day she found herself greatly improved."

The next morning she went out for prayer again. "Even as I went back to my seat, I could feel that the pain and stiffness had gone completely," she told us... and when Lynn returned later that afternoon, it was to discover that the 'cripple' of the day before had just returned from a hockey match. Katie was healed!

> **My life is completely back to normal**

"My life is completely back to normal," Katie told us. "The last time I went to hospital - twelve months ago now - they told me it would be perfectly OK to do anything from pot-holing to mountain-climbing, and although I have no ambitions in that direction, I think they're probably right."

"My doctor's noticed the difference too. At one time, he'd had the job of trying to help me free up my hands, which had become completely locked. Last time I saw him, I squeezed his hand so hard it hurt him!"

"Katie can speak with confidence about healing now," Lynn commented. "She knows God can heal because He did it for her. The illness is just a distant memory now. What lives on is the joy which comes from remembering God's goodness in healing her."

Video Still

Carol Groome, healed of ME which left her unable to work and all but confined to bed for twelve months.

"From the time I was healed, I've never looked back. God's given me my life back!"

15

24 Hours Which Changed My Life

Carol Groome

Trained in neuro-physiology, Carol Groome had spent years testing other people for neurological diseases. MS, epilepsy, trapped nerves, inherited disorders... over fifteen years, she'd seen the lot. Then, seven years ago, she became a victim herself...

"The problem began with frequent upset stomachs, and I started to lose a lot of weight, and was almost permanently exhausted. My glands were also extremely swollen - indeed, but for that, I think doctors might have dismissed the problem as being all in the mind."

"As it was, they suspected toxoplasmosis or glandular fever, but blood tests came out negative, and I was eventually referred to a consultant immunologist."

There was nothing that could be done

"He diagnosed ME. That was the good news - at least I knew what the problem was. The bad news came when he told me there was no point in having any follow-up appointments, because there was nothing which could be done to treat the disease."

"I carried on struggling to work for as long as possible, but after six months it got too much and I had to leave."

"It was a terrible time. I was almost bed-ridden. I couldn't even concentrate enough to be able to read, so there was no way I could look after the house and children - and to cap it all, my GP didn't even believe the ME diagnosis. I got no help at all, and there seemed to be no hope that things would ever get better."

"Then one day I received an information sheet from a self-help group I'd joined. In it there was an article by someone who had been healed of ME at Peniel. I must admit I was sceptical, but I was desperate too -

so I contacted the person concerned, and after a lot of encouragement on his part decided to visit for the weekend."

"By that time I'd been all but confined to bed for twelve months. I could just about get from the bedroom to the bathroom under my own steam, but that was it. Peniel had very kindly made a flat available for the weekend, but I had to be carried downstairs from the flat, and then taken from there into the church in a wheelchair!"

"During the meeting I felt absolutely terrible, and when Bishop Reid prayed for me and told me I was healed, it was a bit difficult to believe it."

"Over the next twenty four hours, however, I began to feel very different. My energy levels started to improve, and I managed to go for a short stroll. By the next day, I was even able to bath myself and wash my hair - the first time I'd been able to do it on my own for a year!"

My energy levels started to improve

"Since then, we've moved to Brentwood so we can come to Peniel regularly. It's wonderful, when local people ask me why we moved, to be able to tell them what happened. The amazing thing is how many of them think that the stories of miracles in the Trumpet Call newspaper are just made up. I'm able to point out that I'm living proof to the contrary!"

God's given me my life back!

"From the time I was healed, I've never looked back. I'm even been able to take up my old job again, working in a local hospital. God's given me my life back!"

"In fact, Carol was not the only one whose life was changed. Her son, desperate to be a vet, but with a severe allergy to animals, was healed of his allergy (See next chapter). There was even a miracle for Carol's carer, Marjory, who was healed of arthritis!

Daniel Groome, no longer allergic to animal fur and looking forward to pursuing his lifelong dream of becoming a vet

16

Mum, I Want To Be A Vet

Daniel Groome

I first came to Peniel Church when I was nine. My mum had been ill with Chronic Fatigue Syndrome for about 18 months and needed a miracle. She came to the church and was healed. Our whole family came back to the church the following week.

Since the age of five I have wanted to be a vet. Unfortunately, I was allergic to animal fur,

> **I was allergic to animal fur**

making this an impossible dream. A few weeks prior to coming to Peniel, I had visited one of my friends who had an old cat. I had been warned not to stroke animals because of my allergy.

However, on this occasion, I was unable to resist the temptation to handle the cat.

My eyes began to swell up so badly that I could not see. My friend's father had to take me home. My house was within 100 metres of their house, but I could not see to walk home. I was coughing and wheezing. That was how bad my allergy was.

When I came to Peniel, Bishop Reid prayed for me. I did not feel any change at the time. It was not until later that day that I realised that I had been healed.

I was able to stroke cats without any allergic reaction

We went for lunch with a family from the church, who owned two cats. I was able to stroke them without any allergic reaction. I was healed!

I was healed!

That was five years ago. I now have a dog, who recently gave birth to five puppies. I have already started visiting veterinary practices for work experience. Being healed has meant that I can live out my dream of becoming a vet! And if God can do it for me, He can do it for you!

Clive Jefferson, instantly healed of crippling back pain which was previously treated by pumping morphine directly into his spine.

17

Jumping For Joy!

Clive Jefferson

"**I** was having morphine pumped constantly into my back, and even then I was in pain. Yet within 30 seconds of being prayed for, I was completely better."

A fifty-year old planning enforcement officer from Worcestershire is confounding the medics following a miracle healing at Brentwood's Peniel Pentecostal Church.

Clive Jefferson told Peniel that he had been forced to retire from his job on health grounds after an accident at work had left him in agony and all but unable to move.

"I'd gone to measure up a site," he explained, "and there was a car in the way. The window was open, so without thinking I leant in, released the brake and pushed it out the way. Two days later, I couldn't walk."

The incident was to mark the start of a desperate twelve months, as doctors drew a blank in their efforts to diagnose and treat him.

"To begin with, my GP sent me along for physiotherapy, Clive told us. The therapist put me on a sort of rack to stretch my back ... and it took four people to get me off again! After that I had just about every kind of investigation you can think of - CAT scans, MRI scans, bone scans, X-rays - but nothing came of it. In fact, the specialist told me that although I appeared to be a fifty-year-old with the back of an eighty-year old, there was basically nothing wrong - though how he had the gall to say it when I could scarcely walk, I don't know. He even accused me of malingering, and threatened to send a video camera round to spy on me. That was the last straw - it was probably just as well for him that I couldn't move!"

Ordinary epidurals did nothing

By the time doctors concluded that two bones in his back had seized up (rather like a nut and bolt, as he puts it), the pain was so severe that drugs could do little to contain it. Ordinary epidurals did nothing to help, and Clive was referred to the national orthopaedic centre in Oswestry. In the meantime, though, he had been fitted up with what he describes as his plumbing system - a small pump on his chest which forced morphine directly into his spine.

There followed a frustrating and fruitless few months as NHS waiting lists left Clive being shunted from one hospital to another, and then yet more problems.

I was visiting my sister in Henley, Clive explains. In the car, my back had been, if anything, even more uncomfortable than usual, and before long there was a swelling the size of an apple where the tube for the morphine entered my spine.

Clive's sister - a nurse - reacted quickly, and Clive was admitted to the Royal Berkshire Hospital, where the initial diagnosis was meningitis. Four days later, he was released again, but badly shaken. The trip to Henley was to mark a turning point, however, as Clive relates.

"One of my sister's fellow church-members had been to Peniel for healing, and had mentioned the place to her. My sister in turn suggested perhaps I ought to come along."

Clive was somewhat reluctant initially, but by this time he had run out of alternatives and was ready to try anything.

"I'd always led an active life, he explained. In thirty three years at work, this was the first real problem I'd had. But by the time I visited my sister I'd been at home for nearly a year. I couldn't walk. My back would lock up half-way upstairs, and I'd be completely stuck. I couldn't bath or shower unaided. I couldn't sleep. I'd lost three stone in weight. I couldn't even read, because the drugs were affecting my vision. There was absolutely nothing I could do - I felt as though the end of the world was coming."

"I'll admit I was a bit dubious about coming to Peniel. It meant a long journey, and I was half expecting something like a Billy Graham crusade, which was bad news as far as I was concerned, but I really was desperate - and when we finally made it, I was very pleasantly surprised. The people were really genuinely friendly, and the whole thing was very down to earth."

He commanded the pain to leave my body... and it did!

"I sat through the singing, and then Bishop Reid came up to me and told me to stand up. I reached automatically for my stick, but he told me to leave it. Then he said he was going to walk backwards and wanted me to walk towards him as he did so. He commanded the pain to leave my body ... and it did just that! Within thirty seconds I went from complete agony to no pain at all - not even an ache. It was scary!"

"I suppose I'd expected that if I was healed at all, it would be a gradual thing. Instead, I felt so completely better, I wanted to run back to Kidderminster!"

Clive may have been convinced, but he faced scepticism at home.

"Friends and neighbours found it hard to believe. My wife probably had the worst job of all, having lived with my problems for over a year. But I think they started to be convinced when I rebuilt the garden wall within a week of coming to Peniel, and then went on to tidy up the entire garden, paint a few ceilings and fix the car!"

"The best part was the reaction of my children. Two days after coming to Peniel, one of my daughters was visiting, and I said to her I've got something to tell you. I watched as an expression of fear came over her face ... and then I got up and ran out of the room! After that we dissolved in tears and hugs - and the tears carried on when I phoned my other daughter to tell her what had happened."

"In fact, I've done an awful lot of crying recently. I think I've become a real Christian at last. God has done something tremendous for me, and I just can't get over it."

John Davies, crippled for 23 years with spondylitis, now completely healed and fighting fit.

18

Crippled No More!

John Davies

By the age of 39, I had been working as a postman for nearly 20 years. Of course, a job like that involves a fair amount of heavy lifting, humping sacks of letters around and so on. However, I had grown used to it, and never gave it a second thought. Not until the day when I lifted up a mailbag and felt a sudden sharp pain in my neck.

That night, the pain developed down my right side and my condition worsened. After months of excruciating agony I eventually became bedridden and was diagnosed as having cervical spondilytis. Every part of me hurt and I had almost become a helpless baby, even at times having to be fed by my wife, as I was unable to hold a cup.

> **I had almost become a helpless baby**

With three young children and my wife at home, my circumstances seemed hopeless. I needed to provide for them, but every time I tried going back to work the pain would make it impossible for me to stay for any length of time and I would be bedridden again within a short time.

During this time I heard about someone who was visiting our town who had a ministry of divine healing. My wife and I attended the meeting and I had hands laid on me. Despite some temporary relief, nothing really changed and although I seemed to go through periods of remission, there was never any lasting improvement. It was even thought that I had multiple sclerosis. During one period of improvement I got a job with a clothing firm, who were very good to me as I still had to have a considerable amount of sick leave and needed transport wherever I went. Even with crutches and other orthopaedic aids, including a wheelchair, my mobility was extremely limited.

It was my wife who bore the brunt of the care and the pressure of bringing up a young family with the added financial strain that my periods out of work brought. I felt so helpless and frustrated at seeing her having to do everything. One day I was watching my wife dig the garden, and I was so desperate that I asked God then to either take me or heal me. Little did I know that my wife had been praying all the time for God to heal me - and firmly believed that He would!

Fifteen years ago, we went to a church where Bishop Reid was ministering. During the meeting he came and spoke to me and I was convinced God was going to heal me then. I was bitterly disappointed that night when nothing seemed to happen, but came to accept that God's grace would be sufficient for me.

A short time later, we came to Peniel for our daughter's wedding. I enjoyed the marriage service and subsequent weekend meetings very much, and my wife and I began to consider moving to the area to become part of the church. One Saturday morning when we had come to Brentwood to look for a flat, I was out shopping with my grandchildren in town when I realised I would have to go home, as the pain in my body was so severe. I felt I would collapse in the street and fall unconscious. That evening, although I did not feel well enough, I went to the meeting with my wife.

In the name of Jesus Christ I command this man to be healed

When we arrived, my wife asked God specifically to heal me that night. Some time into the service, Bishop Reid called both of to the front. He laid hands on me and said, "In the name of Jesus

Christ I command this man to be healed." I felt at that moment as though a red hot sword had gone down my spine and there was what seemed like a hard kick in the small of my back. In fact, it felt as though my back was broken. I fell to the floor and then jumped up.

When I realised I had jumped up, I knew I was healed. I looked at my hands which had been twisted with arthritic pain, and they were quite normal. I started to walk back to my seat and realised I was not limping. The words came to me then - "You are healed - the pain is not going to come back and you are going to forget it." And that is exactly what has happened.

I have had no recurrence of the pain and I even find it hard to remember exactly what it was like, despite having endured it for 23 years. That night I went back to my daughter's house. I ran up the stairs, something I could never have done before. What was even more amazing was that I picked up my 23 year old daughter up and swung her around. I had never been able to pick her up in her life before.

When I returned home to Wales, I found many people could not believe what had happened to me, and they thought it would not last! The very next day I returned all the surgical and orthopaedic appliances that I had acquired over the years - an orthopaedic chair, bath and crutches. The authorities wanted me to keep them, but I knew God had said it would not come back, and I knew it wouldn't. It has now been 13 years since my healing, and I

> **I knew God had said it would not come back**

walk every day and feel so fit and full of energy. Every day gratefulness to God wells up in my heart and brings tears to my eyes as I realise how faithful He has been to me.

Urmila Raval, totally healed of terminal cancer and living a normal life.

19

Healed From Cancer

Urmila Raval
by Doctor Juan Esquivel

Carcinoma of the breasts is now the most common lethal cancer in women. In this disease, the hopes of a cure rest on early recognition and prompt treatment. In the case of Urmila Raval, diagnosis had indeed been made early, but she declined treatment, and by the time she visited Peniel Church, she was close to death. This is the account of a miraculous healing after Christian prayer, as witnessed by a medical doctor.

In the second week of May, 1991, Urmila Raval came for the first time to Peniel Church. Six years earlier, she had noticed a small lump on one breast. She had been examined by doctors, who diagnosed cancer of the breast and recommended surgical removal. Urmila refused to follow their advice and instead tried homeopathy for some time.

As time went by, she started to lose weight. She just wasn't hungry any more and developed a persistent cough and pain in her side. She eventually went back to the hospital, where x-rays confirmed that the cancer spread to the lungs.

When Urmila visited the Church, she had not eaten for months. I can remember her well, coming up for prayer. Her face and arms were characteristic of the terminal cancer cases I had seen in my early years of medical training. It was easy to delineate her bones since there was not much more than a thin layer of skin covering them.

She had come because she had heard that the daughter of a friend had been healed of severe asthma, and even though she was not a Christian herself, she felt that she had nothing to lose. This was a last resort. She knew that she could not find the answer in Hinduism.

The next time she visited the Church, Bishop Reid asked me to examine her. He always said that miracles should stand up to medical scrutiny and this one was no exception. She was a transformed person. The pain had gone and she had started to put on weight. Urmila later told me, "When I came that day, I could not walk or sit without pain. Sleeping had become almost impossible. Then I went home. Little by little I started to walk easily, and that same day I felt like eating. I was not able to eat much at first, but little by little I started eating more."

Naturally, her stomach capacity had decreased because of the long period of fasting and it limited the amount of food she could ingest.

Three months later she had gone back to her normal weight, and to her surprise, the lump had completely disappeared.

She was last examined in January, 1992, when the doctors screened her, looking for evidence of cancer. The scan revealed no bone metastasis (distant spread) and the chest x-rays were clear. They asked her to continue to attend the Outpatient Department after what they described as a remarkable recovery from her condition.

Urmila said that she felt better than ever before. When she told her friends in the Hindu community what happened, they couldn't deny what they saw. Some even came to the meetings asking for prayer, and some keep coming. One of her friends, Malti, said, "God has touched us all and there is something special that keeps bringing us here. We know that Jesus can heal and we follow Him now."

Like so many of the other cases which Bishop Reid has asked me to examine, there was not only a physical recovery, but also a mental and spiritual one. It has been a thrill to have the opportunity to take a close look at the healings God has done in our church.

My medical and scientific background often makes me sceptical of the possibility of blind eyes being opened, crippled people walking, chronic conditions being instantly healed. Nonetheless I have seen it happen time and time again, and having had the opportunity to examine these cases, I can only wonder in amazement.

The Son of God is still available to do the same things recorded in the Gospels 2000 years ago - not only to heal, but to give us a better and more abundant life.

A Visit That Will Change Your Life

Peniel Pentecostal Church - A Church where healing and miracles happen today. Come and see what God can do for you!

Regular Meetings:

Every Tuesday & Friday at 7.30pm, Sundays at 10.00am where Bishop Michael Reid ministers and prays for the sick

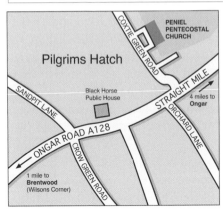

M25: Exit 28. Take A1023 to Brentwood. Continue along High St to double roundabout (Wilson's Corner). Turn left, then follow map.

A12: Leave at M25 junction. Then as above.

A127: Leave at A128 junction. Take A128 to Brentwood. Continue to double roundabout (Wilson's Corner). Go straight on, then follow map.

A13: Take A128 to Brentwood, then as above.

Peniel Pentecostal Church, 49 Coxtie Green Road
Pilgrims Hatch, Brentwood, Essex, CM14 5PS, England.
Tel: +44 (0)1277 372996 Fax: +44 (0)1277 375046
www.peniel.org

The Peniel Choir

Peniel Choir supports the ministry of Bishop Reid and Peniel Pentecostal Church, and appears regularly with the Bishop on television and at various venues in the UK and Europe. These choristers energetically sing of the love of God that has touched their lives. Through their singing you will be: INSPIRED with hope that what God has done for them he can do for you; CHALLENGED to examine your life in the light of the simple truth of the Gospel; & IGNITED with the faith of God for yourself. You can hear the choir every Sunday at the 10am service, at publicised special events, and on their four albums which are available from the Church Bookshop and by mail order from Alive UK.

"The Peniel Choir have that rare gift of breathing the love of Christ into every note of their singing. The conviction that Jesus is Lord in each member's life shines through all they do. And what a truly, inspirational sound that lifts the spirit and brings glory to God! I can't wait to hear them again!"

Phillip Billson, Producer, BBC Religion.

Music & Miracles

Combining the inspiration of the Peniel Choir with the clear-cut presentation of the gospel, All Churches Music & Miracles has become established as an integral part of our outreach to the community.

Many who would not normally enter a church have come and witnessed the miracle power of God impacting on their own lives or on the lives of others.

Meetings are held monthly on Sunday evenings at 6.30pm throughout the year.

EVERYONE IS WELCOME!

Miracle Conferences

Visitors from all over the world travel to Peniel Church for the annual Miracle Conferences, held over the Easter and August Bank Holiday Weekends.

Bishop Michael Reid and other dynamic international speakers minister from the Word of God and pray for the sick, and the Peniel Choir ministers in song.

So come and see Jesus' Miracle Working Power.
He's here for you, whatever your need is!

*For further information and dates, call +44 (0)1277 372996
or visit our website www.peniel.org*

Peniel Academy

A School With A Difference

In 1998 Peniel Pentecostal Church purchased Brizes Park to cater for the expansion of Peniel Academy, the church's day school. The premises were part of God's consistent miracle provision for the Academy which was started with 17 pupils in 1982.

Brizes Park is a listed mansion set in 74 acres with a courtyard, walled garden, swimming pool, tennis courts, and over thirty classrooms. The school admits pupils aged between 5 and 18 whose parents are committed to the work of the church and its christian ethos emphasises the watchword "excellence" in all that it does. Each child is unique and the school's comprehensive co-educational structure caters for all abilities with the accent on being relevant, practical and seeking to fulfil each individual's full potential.

Through the dedication of its Christian staff, the school's academic performance has been exemplary, frequently ranking amongst the highest in the country for GCSE and A level results. The majority of pupils go on to further education and achieve top quality degrees, ensuring a firm platform for their chosen career.

In its chosen sport of table tennis, the school often supplies players for England teams at different age groups on the international scene. Within the English schools team competition, the school often secures the majority of trophies available at various ages, highlighting its position as one of the top schools in the country.

School members have appeared on "Blue Peter" and the junior choir came runner up in Radio Two's national "Minstrels in the Gallery" singing competion.

The aim of the school is to educate children, within the context of God's principles of life, so that they can be an influence for good in the community and nation. As the miracles of God sustain the school, so the pupils themselves grow up in an environment where miracles are expected. God enriches each part of the children's lives - body, mind and soul. As the children progress, the Lord faithfully adds them to become functioning members of His church worldwide.

Parents and pupils gather together on the first day of a new term at their new school.

Peniel College Of Higher Education

Peniel College of Higher Education was founded as a result of a unique affiliation agreement with Oral Roberts University, making it the only campus in the United Kingdom authorised by ORU and the North Central Accrediting Association to offer ORU degree courses.

At PCHE we believe that practical Biblical study will equip and prepare you for ministry and mission, but more importantly for life. Our courses are therefore open to people from all walks of life who share the common purpose of impacting their individual worlds with the dynamic message of the gospel.

Students at PCHE study in a Christian atmosphere. Our resident faculty are mature Christian scholars who have proved the miracle power of Christ in every aspect of their lives. They will share their expertise in ministry, education and professional life.

We challenge students to reach their full potential in the areas of spirit, mind and body. We encourage success in their careers, their communities and their family life, founded on the Holy Spirit and sustained by a steadfast reliance on Christian principles.

A graduate from Peniel College of Higher Education will not only be equipped with academic qualifications but with a clear work ethic, a sense of responsibility and purpose and an unwavering adherence to Christian truths in all areas of life.

If you have been thinking of studying for a really worthwhile degree, either to prepare for some form of Christian ministry or as an individual Christian interested in developing yourself academically and spiritually, this is the College for you.

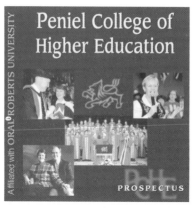

Fully accredited degree courses are available on a full or part-time basis.

For a free brochure or more information about PCHE courses:

Call:	+44 (0)1277 372996
Fax:	+44 (0)1277 375332
Email:	che@peniel.org
Website:	www.peniel.org

Alive UK

Alive UK publishes a wide selection of inspirational books, videos, music and ministry audio cassettes and CDs. Alive UK is also a UK distributor of books by world renowned evangelist, Dr TL Osborn.

For a full product list:

Call: +44 (0)1277 373436
Fax: +44 (0)1277 375578
Email: aliveuk@peniel.org

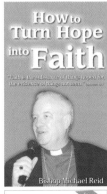

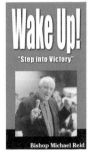